Rafael López-Pedraza

Cult

CW00662631

Rafael López-Pedraza

Cultural Anxiety

DAIMON
VERLAG

Acknowledgements:

I would like to thank Fiona Cairns, Ruth Horine, Robert Hinshaw and Valerie López for their generous editorial contributions to the essays comprising this book, and Michael Heron for his translating of the Duende and Consciousness of Failure papers.

R. L.-P.

The chapter "Moon Madness – Titanic Love" originally appeared in the book, *Images of the Untouched*, edited by Joanne Stroud and Gail Thomas (Spring, Dallas, 1982) and we are grateful to Spring Publications for making it available. "Cultural Anxiety" was delivered as a paper at the Ninth International Congress of Analytical Psychology in Jerusalem in 1983. It was subsequently published in the official Congress Proceedings, *Symbolic and Clinical Approaches in Practice and Theory,* edited by Luigi Zoja and Robert Hinshaw (Daimon, Zurich, 1986). Both essays were updated for the present publication. "Reflections on the Duende" and "Consciousness of Failure" were translated from Spanish by Michael Heron and appear here in English for the first time.

Cover design by Hanspeter Kälin; we thank Pro Litteris, Zurich, and the heirs of Pablo Picasso for permission to use a detail from Pablo Picasso's "Guernica" as a cover illustration, copyright © 1990 PRO LITTERIS, Zurich; we thank Edy Gonzales for the back cover photo of Rafael López-Pedraza.

ISBN 3-85630-520-3

TABLE OF CONTENTS

FOREWORD

This small collection of essays is the product of my reflections on two aspects of human nature, two aspects that I consider to be in exclusive opposition to each other. One aspect is our access to archetypal images and consistent life-forms, making possible psyche, emotions and feeling values, and marking our inner processes. The other is a lack of images, a vacuum, a lacuna, out of which come excess and the madness of power.

Not only have these two aspects of human nature been involved in a constant struggle throughout man's history on earth, but I am aware of their struggle in my own life and relationships, and they have become central to my conception of psychotherapy.

Let me advise the reader that in the following exposition I try not to qualify these two opposites. My position is psychic and therapeutic, grounded in the way our psychic entity is aware of these two opposites and learns how to suffer their irreconcilability.

The material in the essays is taken mostly from literature, poetry and historical events, but it is reinforced by my own practice of psychotherapy. I hope the reader will appreciate that, in general, I have kept the language of the essays as simple as possible, sometimes even rather colloquial, to avoid the melée of the schools of psychology and even Jungian semantics. In doing so I have given, I think, easier access to the images with which I am dealing.

MOON MADNESS – TITANIC LOVE
A MEETING OF PATHOLOGY AND POETRY

This paper is concerned with two elements of great psychological importance in today's psychotherapy. The first is the psychology of the virginal as it is reflected in the strange relationship between the mythological figure of Endymion and the Moon, a myth which has attracted many poets and writers.[1] Endymion is presented as being in love with the Moon, a love which indicates a complex psychology, its spectrum ranging from poetic creativity to a severe pathology. It is a love which gives Endymion a very special and sometimes peculiar relationship to virginity. The Moon is in the guise of Selene, a Titaness, personifying the titanic level of the psyche, the second element with which we shall be concerned. In the four essays of this book, I shall refer to several strange aspects of human nature, which I attribute to the psychology of the Titans. I consider Titanism to represent a very important aspect of human nature which has not yet been fully explored.

There seems to have been no cult of the Titans. Titanic times can be viewed as a sort of transitional period between primitive man and cultured, civilized man, a period during which there was neither the ritual and cult of primitive man nor the well-defined anthropomorphic imagery of the highly cultured and religious man. Now, just as we all have primitive complexes within us so well worked out by Jungian psychology, we must

---

1. Helen H. Law, *Bibliography of Greek Myth in English Poetry*, Bulletin XXVII (Oxford, Ohio: American Classical League, 1955), p. 15. Under *Endymion*, forty-two poets are listed.

all have, implicitly, a Titanic level of the psyche – Titanic
complexes – though these have not yet been explicitly worked
out. A more differentiated psychology at this Titanic level is
still waiting to be tackled. There are personalities in which the
Titanic seems to predominate and odd behaviors and pathologies which, I believe, can only be evaluated in terms of
Titanism, something I shall refer to in more detail later. I
believe the psychology of the Titan is extremely important, particularly if we accept that the Titanic ingredient exists in all of
us.

First, allow me to clarify somewhat the mythological field in
which the image on which we shall be focusing resides. But in
order to clear the ground for a clearer idea of the Titanic, we
need first to take a look at what it is not. The Titans belong to
the mythological time of Kronos, the time of the first and second generations of the Gods. This was the time before Zeus
waged war on his Titanic progenitors and brought about a new
order, ritual, religion, culture and civilization. Zeus' new world
also brought about a differentiation of images, what Nilsson
calls the Greek anthropomorphism in mythology and history.
Nilsson and other modern scholars agree that it took about a
millennium to realize this anthropomorphism. During those
hidden centuries of the Greek Dark Ages, it was the task of
bards and minstrels – the poets, in other words – to sing the
same songs over and over again, to repeat the Mycenaean
heroic sagas: that is, the mythologized history of the Heroes.
And as the poets sang, they wove a net which, little by little,
caught the images of a divine mythology. Into this net of repeated tales they wove the Gods and Goddesses as living anthropomorphic images. This was how the clarity of the well-
differentiated, *consistent* image was created. Moreover, as
Nilsson states,

> during the Dark Ages between the fall of the Mycenaean cul-
> ture and the Homeric period – the time when the specifically
> Greek anthropomorphism must have been developed – it is to
> be presumed that the *internal* anthropomorphism was the lead-
> ing force. . . . For we have been educated by the Greeks to a

consistent anthropomorphism and this is something specifically Greek.[2]

Today, we can be educated once again by the Greeks – their mythology offering the constant possibility of a Renaissance in the psyche. We have been educated by the Greeks; for the sake of precision, I would add, by the Greek *poets*. I consider this education to be an education of the soul. It is a psychical education. And this education of the soul through poetry – poetical, mythological anthropomorphism – is the reservoir from which Western man can draw to educate and perpetually recreate his soul.[3]

Hölderlin wrote: "Full of merit, yet poetically man dwells on earth."[4] With this line, the poet tells us that our education today contains both what man does by merit and by poetical intervention. In order to reflect the image which I shall be elaborating, we shall need both merit and poetry.

But let us get back to the Titans. Unfortunately, we know very little about them. The *Titanomachia* and two-thirds of Aeschylus' trilogy on Prometheus have been lost, but for our purposes her, scholars of mythology give us an adequate image of the ancient race of Gods. Here is what Kerényi has to say of the Titans:

> The stories of the Titans are about gods who belong to such a distant past that we know them only from tales of a particular kind, and only as exercising a particular function. The name of

---

2. Martin P. Nilsson, *History of Greek Religion,* trans. F.J. Fielden (New York: W.W. Norton, 1964), pp. 143-44.
3. To educate the soul is the concern of many Jungian analysts of the present generation. Soul-making is one of the main themes of the writings of James Hillman. See especially, *Re-Visioning Psychology* (New York: Harper Colophon Books, 1977); also Robert Sardello's excellent paper, *Educating with Soul,* published by The Center for Civic Leadership, The University of Dallas, Irving, Texas.
4. Taken from Martin Heidegger, *Hölderlin y la Escencia de la Poesía,* trans. Juan D. García Bacca (Merida: Universidad de los Andes, 1968), p. 15.

> Titan has, since the most ancient times, been deeply associated
> with the divinity of the Sun, and seems originally to have been
> the supreme title of beings who were, indeed, celestial gods,
> but gods of very long ago, still savage and subject to no laws.[5]

Kerényi gives us a general picture of the psychology of the
Titans: no laws, no order, no limits. In his extraordinary work
on on particular Titan, Prometheus, Kerényi named him "the
archetype of human existence,"[6] though he was careful to say
that he wished to avoid the philosophical connotation of
Existentialism in his use of the word "existence." However, it
was his conception of Prometheus as the archetype of human
existence, as well as what we see of Titanism under the magnifying glass in the works of some of the masters of modern literature, that sparked my insights into Titanism as it appears in
our time. In my opinion, Kerényi, a great pioneer who made the
connection between the excess of the Titans and human existence, was, despite what he says, undoubtedly under the twofold
influence of Jung's research on archetypes and the ideas and
literature inspired by Existentialism. These ideas, in a man who
was a war exile, must have helped to make possible his *Prometheus,* a textbook study which introduces the difficult psychology of the Titans and which gave me a point of departure
for my own reflections.[7]

For didactic purposes, we can say that, just as the Greeks
thought of the Titanic times as the reign in earlier times of more
savage celestial Gods, in the ontogenesis of man, there have
also been Titanic times. Our adolescence probably contains a
large element of Titanism – excess, unboundedness, lawless-
ness, chaos, barbarism and so on. We can add this Titanic element to the Puer's celestial trip, which exhibits its own form of

5. Carl Kerényi, *The Gods of the Greeks,* trans. Norman Cameron
   (London: Thames and Hudson, 1976), p. 20.
6. See Kerényi, *Prometheus: Archetypal Image of Human Existence,*
   trans. Ralph Mannheim (London: Thames and Hudson, 1963).
7. For me, the archetypes and human existence are the two fields for
   study. My interest is to enlarge a bit the beachhead which pioneers
   such as Kerényi have established.

excess, lack of limitation and destructiveness.[8] My own reflections of Titanism have grown out of the recollections of my own life, from living in Titanic societies which, psychologically, could be said to be sandwiched between primitive and civilized man. They come also from observing excess everywhere in today's life, in even the most highly differentiated societies whose traditions are based on the High Religion – an excess which is most evident in the missionary zeal predominating in all facets of life. Western civilization is becoming more and more Titanic. My reflections however come, above all, from my practice, dealing with patients whose psychology makes sense only if one can detect the Titanic element – what Jung and others might call simply shadow or unconscious – and appreciate just how Titanic they are in spite of their highly articulate and cultured self-expression.

For me, to be unconscious is to be unconscious of the archetypes, either in history or in a lifetime; to equate Titanism with the unconscious, then, is quite another business. For instance, with these patients, the motto that I have adopted – "The image, what makes possible the impossible"[9] – simply does not work. To 'make possible' is to 'make conscious' an image that has been 'impossible.' These patients, however, are unable to form an image; or just when one thinks an image is in process, something coming from nowhere destroys any such possibility. Sometimes, one can see that when they offer what could be called an image, there are no accompanying psychical feelings or creativity. What one is taking as an image which could move psyche is, for them, a stereotype, a mimetism. Titanism can also be detected in what Jungian psychology has called 'the Intellectual.' There is an intellectual approach to the image, an approach which requires a magnifying glass when a

8. Marie-Louise von Franz already saw something similar in her discussion of the Puer in connection with Bruno Goetz's *Reich ohne Raum*. However, where she saw only the Puer, I am suggesting also the presence of a Titanic element.
9. José Lezama Lima, "Las Imágenes Posibles" in *Esferaimagen* (Barcelona: Tusquets Editor, 1970), p. 51ff.

dream is intellectualized. (One wonders whether the method of amplification feeds intellectualism.) Let us push this Titanic element even further. Kerényi's view of the Titans, that they represent a particular function, is perhaps what I am trying to get at concerning this Titanic ingredient which exists in us all. However, we are faced here with a difficulty; a function suggests something specific, whereas Titanism seems so disparate and wild.

I have already mentioned the well-defined Gods and Goddesses with their *consistent* images; in other words, the archetypes. Nilsson again: "Anthropomorphism has, therefore, a characteristic *limitation*."[10] If that is so, it is difficult to see the Titans (whose main characteristic is excess) as archetypes with their own inherent limitation, and even more difficult to see them as the images of an archetype. Furthermore, Nilsson states: "The Titans are abstractions or empty names of whose significance we cannot judge."[11] So to call the Titans archetypes, or even representatives of a particular function, is a bit risky.[12] Nevertheless, in poetry and iconography the Titans *are* personified, represented as forms, enabling us, perhaps, to broaden our view of anthropomorphism and imagine the forms of the Titans as a sort of borderline anthropomorphism. Personally, I prefer to view them as mythological *figures* representing mimicry and excess, for they are not archetypal configurations. In order to gain insight into this mimetism, jargon and excess, we need a strong archetypal training and point of view; it is only by having those well-defined forms as a background that we can have insight into what is, by definition, formless in human nature.

Kerényi wrote *Prometheus* in 1946, just after the Second World War when, it seems, man began to be aware of hitherto

10. Nilsson, p. 144.
11. *Ibid.*, p. 23.
12. If we were to follow Kerényi on this point and agree that the Titans represent a particular function, then the Titans, with their excessiveness, could be called the archetype of excess.

unknown aspects of himself, as if the war had forced him to reflect on some estranged parts of himself. We have the literature running from Camus' *The Outsider,* published during the war (in 1942), to Anthony Burgess' *A Clockwork Orange,* to confirm this impression.[13] I connect what Camus and Burgess expressed in their novels, in terms of mythology and Archetypal Psychology, with the Titanic level in man which we have been tracking: no laws, no order, no limits – in short, excess. Once again, it is literature which has opened the door to an exploration (which we in psychology are just beginning) of those levels in man where the Titan lurks. But, following Kerényi again, we have to accept that, in the history of human life, the Titanic expresses itself where we are excessive. In this sense, the Titanic could be, if not an archetype, then a particular function.

Let me return to Nilsson's statement about the Titans whom, as you recall, he terms "abstractions or empty names of whose significance we cannot judge."[14] Careful thought about this statement offers us another point of reflection giving us a wider view of Titanism. We are all inhabited by these abstractions, these empty names; we are flooded in our daily lives by empty names – our daily "blah-blah-blah" – not to mention our psychotherapy, in which, if we are unaware of our Titanism, we can fall into empty jargon, even when using the most beautiful words. Our psychotherapy can become empty names – Titanic jargon. There are areas in our psyches, in our lives, in which we have no reflection because there are no images and so no feelings to judge. Keeping in mind these two basic elements of Titanism – its emptiness on the one hand, its excess on the other – we can begin to evaluate excess throughout our history, our life and our practice. Our challenge is to bring reflection to that which has no limits, to that which is not archetypal, to that

13. In discussing modern manifestations of the Titanic, I would like to stay within the containers of *The Outsider* and *A Clockwork Orange* (which I presume most everyone has read).
14. See Note 11.

which, paradoxically, cannot be reflected because it has no images – though it can be detected through its own Titanic rhetoric.[15]

Now, Nilsson's statement that the Titans are "abstractions or empty names" enables us to push our inquiry in another direction, that of our so-called lacunae: that which we cannot know or grasp in ourselves, those empty abstractions, the nothings, the holes – those black holes which seem to fascinate everyone just now. No archetypes, these, but holes. If we can contain both the emptiness and the excess, we are in a better position to be aware of the Titanic. The excess could even grow out of the emptiness, the lacunae.

This discussion of the Titans should, I hope, aid us in Archetypal Psychology to acquire a basic idea of the field they offer for study. It would be a pity, after all, if Archetypal Psychology became no more than the study of the archetypes, depicting merely the characteristic profiles of Artemis, Aphrodite, Mars and so on. The most important element of the Titan – the excess, which, as far as I can see, emerges from the emptiness – leads, among other things, into pathology or 'odd behavior': the excess that history and all of us are filled with.

I have leaned rather heavily on Kerényi and Nilsson, but, as far as I know, Kerényi was the first to approach Titanism in depth, and Nilsson's contribution adds tremendously to our insights. As you know, there is little mention of the Titans in Jungian psychology. What little there is is found in the old Orphic Platonic connections between the Titans and the evil in human nature. As Dodds points out, "Plato, in his *Laws,* referred to people 'who show off the old Titan nature,' and to impulses which are 'neither of man nor of God' ":[16] that is to say, in Jungian terms, the evil in our shadow which we cannot

---

15. We have to realize that there are two kinds of rhetoric: the archetypal and the Titanic. The Titanic rhetoric can be detected in references such as, "That is mere rhetoric."
16. E.R. Dodds, *The Greeks and the Irrational* (Berkeley: University of California Press, 1968), p. 156.

integrate and so have to reject. Certainly, Jungian psychology has not allowed modern literature and imagery of our times to provide a reflection of this part of nature which is usually called 'existence,' and which I equate with Titanism.

I now return to Camus and Burgess. From the very first lines of *The Outsider,* we are given an extraordinary picture of *emptiness* (lacuna or void, if you like). The Outsider receives a telegram informing him of his mother's death; but he shows no archetypal reaction – no grief, no sense of loss, for example – to that event. The *excess* in him appears when he shoots an Arab. The first bullet killed the Arab, the following four were excessive. Archetypally speaking, one can be driven by panic to shoot one bullet in a primitive instinctual reaction, but with five bullets, there is an excess. The killing of the Arab helps us to distinguish an archetypally limited situation from one that is not archetypal at all. The cause of the Outsider's undoing is attributed to the Sun – one of the Titanic celestial Gods. This sort of projection of the Outsider's guilt onto something as absurd as the Sun belongs very much to Titanism. With some of my patients, I have had to listen to the most ridiculous projections of guilt, blaming everything except themselves which, for me, is part of the Titanic nature in man.[17] At the end of the book, during a discussion with a priest, Camus shows masterfully the Outsider's inability to form an image. The priest says that prisoners before death often see the Divine on the stone wall of their cells, but the Outsider replies that he has tried to see the face of his girlfriend, Maria, and has failed.

17. I would like to draw attention to this connection between guilt and Titanism as seen from the perspective of Archetypal Psychology. It could be useful. Both the projection of guilt and the carrying of all the guilt upon oneself are Titanic. It is to be noted that, generally speaking, psychotherapy tries to cure the projection by getting the patient to internalize the guilt he so loosely and Titanically projects, and in the second case, by encouraging the patient to blame the parents, society, or whatever. Both are Titanic "solutions" which have nothing to do with a psychotherapy that moves the soul through images.

A Clockwork Orange, extending the theme of the Titanic implicit in Camus' novels, shows total excess everywhere – beatings, killings, rapes and so forth. The whole of society is excess, "savage and subject to no laws," as Kerényi says of the Titans. Religion has become an easy mimesis which the young Titan uses to his own profit.[18] All of society's institutions are based on this same Titanic excess. And psychiatry, with its Titanic Promethean technology, its missionary zeal, tries to resolve the Titanic riddle for the benefit of the poor Titan, society, and humanity as a whole. Psychiatry as the savior. Prometheus, a more sophisticated Titan, appears in many guises, but closest to our concern is his appearance as the savior in the guise of a technological psychiatrist trying to save the Titan.[19]

Psyche does not learn from Titanic excess. In this connection, we need to make a clear distinction between the suffering, humiliation and pain of Psyche – from which psychological learning, knowledge and soul-making, or soul-initiation, can come – and the repetitive suffering of the Titans – that daily nauseating boredom of the existential level of life.

Certainly, the Titanic personality is the greatest challenge for the soul. So many of the modern psychotherapies try to resolve the soul's conflicts in terms of adaptation to life and 'making it' – a Titanic psychotherapy. Though for a patient in whom the Titanic element is more than just an ingredient, whose dominant personality is Titanic, perhaps the only possible psychotherapy would be to push him into success, forcing him to 'make it.' But this approach is a long way from a consciousness that would weaken and make soul.[20] In addition to the *outer* aspects

18. One has only to think of religious cults, like the one led by Jim Jones, or of the Titan Menoetius – whose name means "he whom mortal doom awaits" – to get a sense of the religious zeal which dwells in the Titanic.
19. I should perhaps mention here that this Titanic excess is not only the concern of psychopathology. Titanic excess has also to do with the medical term *stress,* but this medical interest in the Titanic takes us beyond our purposes.
20. Recently I have heard of the very Titanic conception of trying to

of what has been called external 'human existence,' Titanism
can also manifest itself *inwardly,* when excess is inward and so
falls into pathology. We may see this form of Titanism at work
in the story of Endymion and his lunar lover, the Moon
Goddess Selene. Hesiod's *Theogony* informs us (Kerényi's
version):

> The Titaness Theia bore, to her husband Hyperion, Helios, the
> sun, Selene, the moon and Eos, the dawn.[21]

There is not much doubt, then, that the Moon, as Selene, was a
Titaness. And it is within the difficult mythological and psychological fields which we have been discussing that we now come
to the story of Selene and her love for the shepherd Endymion.

> It was told that when Selene disappeared behind the mountain-
> crest of Latmos in Asia Minor, she was visiting her lover
> Endymion, who slept in a cave in that region. Endymion, who
> in all portrayals of him is shown as a beautiful youth, a herds-
> man or hunter, received the gift of everlasting sleep – doubt-
> less, in the original story, from the moon-goddess herself, so
> that she could always find him and kiss him in his cave.[22]

I would like us to stay with this picture of Selene going down
into the cave to make love with Endymion whenever she wants,
to stay with this image *just as it is.* My interest is to read the
image, not to synthesize it or amplify its components – Moon as
mother, cave as womb and so on.[23]

Now, as Kerényi informs us, the name "Endymion means
one who 'finds himself *within,*' encompassed by his beloved as

"cure" psychosis (a broken archetype) by pushing the patient into psychopathy, pushing the patient into the mimetic Titanic world.
21. Kerényi, *The Gods of the Greeks,* p. 22.
22. *Ibid.,* p. 198.
23. It is clear from Kerényi's account that Selene reserves the right to
make the first move towards Endymion; the shepherd is depicted as
reclining passively and awaiting her amorous advance. Walter Otto
adds that it is characteristic of Titanesses to make the first move in an
erotic encounter.

if in a common garment."[24] We can now begin to imagine what the name Endymion, "the one who finds himself within," might mean. At the most obvious level, it is common enough to say of someone: "Oh yes, so-and-so is a very nice person, but all his energy seems to be inside of him." Or: "It seems to me, so-and-so has a lot of things inside, but he doesn't seem to be able to come out with them." We have all heard this sort of comment about a friend, for example, or a student. And I am sure we can all remember a time in our own lives when whatever we had was only inside, and how we had to wait for it to become something more as our life unfolded. In addition to the meaning of his name as translated by Kerényi, there is another level at which we can reflect upon Endymion living in a cave with the Moon Selene as his lover. For it would seem that Endymion's love with the Moon – who, though a Titaness, is nevertheless a Virgin – keeps him untouched by any other God or Goddess: that is, by other possibilities of life. He remains loyal to his love with the Moon as Selene. We could say that Endymion is a forerunner of Hippolytus, another mythological figure who loved only the Moon – in his case, the Moon as Artemis, a well-defined and consistent image. Endymion is encompassed by his beloved as if by a common garment, which is perhaps to say that he is one who keeps himself virginal. In any case, I think we can connect this inner excess, which we have seen with the story of Endymion and the Titaness Selene, with a peculiar kind of virginity and with a pathology, in contrast to the Titans, whose excess is external.

The imagination of the poet Lycophron was stimulated to create a variation of the love-story of Endymion. In Lycophron's account, according to Kerényi, "the god Hypnos, the winged god of sleep, fell in love with Endymion. He gave the youth the ability to sleep with open eyes."[25] This account greatly enriches the complexities of Endymion. We have all, I believe, in certain moments – far more frequently than we are

24. Kerényi, *The Gods of the Greeks,* p. 198.
25. *Ibid.*

aware – slept through life with open eyes; it is a peculiar lunar state of inner excess. And we can all remember that long period of our youth when we slept with open eyes, endlessly 'mooning around,' to the despair of ourselves and others. Even now, when we want to listen most attentively to an interesting lecture, for example, the God of sleep appears to us and makes us sleep a little. I still do a little sleeping with open eyes myself, some-times during the most interesting moments of my practice! It can also happen that the reality we have before us, a situation which really hits us, can be so overwhelming that we simply go to sleep with open eyes in front of that event. We retreat inside ourselves.

Kerényi relates that according to another poet, Apollonius, Endymion's eternal sleep was "a gift from Zeus, who had per-mitted him to choose his own manner of death: with the result that Endymion had chosen perpetual sleep instead of death."[26] At this point, we can begin to appreciate how these three ac-counts of Endymion's story cited by Kerényi give us some insight into the psychological levels I have been hinting at. In the complexities surrounding Endymion, we find, besides the Moon, the figures of Hypnos, Zeus and death. Of the three accounts, perhaps Apollonius' is the richest and propitiates a deeper psychological view, for Apollonius describes in Endymi-on a serious pathological condition. In Apollonius' version we have a more profound element; Zeus, the eternal father, intervenes, and the appearance of death turns Endymion's story into a 'serious business.' It is as if Apollonius' imagination shows us Zeus playing *fatefully* with a mortal, as the Gods like to do. Zeus grants Endymion the right to choose the manner of his own death. The theme of choosing one's own manner of death has haunted some poets – especially the Romantics. The idea of choosing one's own way of dying could be seen as hav-ing a Titanic, Romantic inflation, coupled with an avoidance of the constant reflection which death plays alongside life – the value of life that comes from the reflection of death. Here we

26. *Ibid.*

directly confront Endymion's pathology, for we can begin to imagine the Endymion mythologem in terms of a serious illness. By having Endymion choose perpetual sleep instead of death, Apollonius is diagnosing, so to speak, the condition of one who has turned the 'death reflection' into a peculiar madness – a condition similar to the one which the German psychiatrist Karl Kahlbaum observed and diagnosed much later in the nineteenth century. In 1874, Kahlbaum coined the word *catatonia* to describe

> that condition in which the patient sits quietly or completely mute and motionless, immovable, with a staring countenance, the eyes fixed on a distant point and apparently completely without volition, without any reaction to sensory impressions, sometimes with a full-fledged cerea flexibilitas as in catalepsy.[27]

Can one not view this description of a schizophrenic symptom as the picture of Endymion, lying in a cave, sleeping his perpetual sleep with open eyes, and waiting for the kisses of the Moon, the Titaness Selene?

This state of being, which Kahlbaum described by means of the empirical method (by merit) was described by the classical poets, the mythographers of antiquity, with the same precision needed for psychiatric diagnosis, using the beauty of poetry compiled into images – an education of the soul. I cannot imagine that poets like Lycophron or Apollonius had not to some extent experienced in their own bodies something of this lunatic state, conceiving it as the love of the young shepherd Endymion, with the Moon, the Titaness Selene. Indeed, all this sleeping in the cave with Selene, this 'mooning around,' is probably part of poetical activity. These poets of antiquity could be said to have had a corporeal lunatic insight. They were able to find themselves within. And it is the recovery of this very corporeal, or psycho-physical, aspect that has been the aim of this paper.

---

27. Lawrence C. Kolb, *Modern Clinical Psychiatry,* eighth edition (London: W.B. Saunders Co., 1973), p. 309.

In twentieth-century poetry – and I shall not be referring to poetical re-creations of Endymion – Endymion has appeared in a quite different way: namely, in the *attitudes, explorations* and the *poetical retinas* of some contemporary poets. André Breton, the great pontiff of Surrealism, wrote in 1928:

> Now I recall Robert Desnos in that epoch that those of us who knew it called *the epoch of dreams.* He "sleeps" but writes and talks. It is night and we are in the studio of my house above the Cabaret Heaven. Outside someone shouts, "Come on, let's go to the Black Cat!" And Desnos goes on seeing what I do not see, what I can only see to the extent he shows it to me.[28]

As is well known, the Surrealists, flourishing in that period *l'entre deux guerres,* were keenly interested in the subconscious. They read a bit of Freud, a bit of alchemy, and a bit about magic. They were steeped in literature. But above all, they were much attracted to Janet's 'Psychic Automatism.' In the first of the Surrealists' many Manifestos, Breton equated Surrealism with Psychic Automatism. He defined Surrealism as "pure psychic automatism by which it is proposed to express, either verbally, or in any other manner, the real functioning of thought," or "the dictation of thought in the absence of any control exercised by reason, beyond aesthetic or moral preoccupations."[29] Some of them developed an automatic writing technique from Janet's discovery. They believed they were writing very profound poems by picking up deep messages from the subconscious. I wonder, though, whether these Surrealists knew that at that time, not so very far from Paris, people were working on the theory of the complexes, one of psychology's deepest and most far-reaching theories: how the complexes – those pieces of history – function in us, sometimes automatically. It

28. André Breton, *Najda* (Mexico: Edition Joaquin Mortiz, 1963), p. 22. This and later passages in English are my own translations from the Spanish.
29. Breton, "Primer Manifiesto," in *Manifiestos del Surrealismo* (Madrid: Ediciones Guadarrama, S.A., 1974), p. 44.

can be said that Janet's discovery was a forerunner of the more serious theory of the complexes.

In addition to their approach to poetry through automatic writing, the Surrealists wrote a lot about the 'Chance Encounter.' Lautréamont's phrase, "as beautiful as the chance meeting upon a dissecting table of a sewing machine and an umbrella,"[30] became one of the pillars of Surrealism. At the same time, however, as they deepened their fascination with the 'Chance Encounter,' there were other people, again, not so very far from Paris, who under the guidance of Richard Wilhelm were studying the theory of synchronicity which he had brought back from China.

Now let us return to Breton's recollection of an evening with Desnos. The scene is captured in a photograph of Desnos lying on a couch in a room above Montparnasse, telling Breton what he is seeing, and creating poetry. I cannot resist connecting him with the image of Endymion, lying sprawled in the beams of the Moon. One can almost see Desnos slipping psycho-physically into the mythologem of Endymion, in love with the Moon – and obviously with poetry, too. Desnos, whom Breton called "the one among us, who is nearest to the Surrealist truth,"[31] *free-associating,* poetically, from the most autonomous parts of his complexes, keeping himself virginal – encompassed with his beloved as if in a common garment – and untouched by other complexes other than this virginal one. At that very moment, somebody in the street below shouts, "Let's go to the Black Cat!" And Breton integrates that shout into his meeting with Desnos as a 'Chance Encounter,' or, if you prefer, a synchronistic event.

Antonio Machado, a great Spanish poet, died in France just a month-and-a-half after the end of the Spanish Civil War, and only two days after the death of his mother. The last image we have of him during his life is of him sitting in a car with his

30. J.H. Matthews, *An Introduction to Surrealism* (University Park, Pennsylvania: The Pennsylvania State University Press, 1965), p. 105.
31. Breton, "Primer Manifiesto," *Manifiestos del Surrealismo,* p. 48.

mother on his knees as they cross the Spanish border into France. According to a friend of mine who was one of his disciples, Machado used to walk in a very peculiar way, which drew everyone's attention. It seems as if he had some problem with the movement of his body, since he walked in a way that could be described (following Kahlbaum) as catatonic. His living experience of the catatonic was evident in his shuffling steps.

In his book, *Juan de Mairena,* Machado introduced *"el paleto perfecto,"* one of those Castilian peasants, with weathered, wrinkled face, wearing a black beret, simple shirt, waistcoat, corduroy trousers and *alpargatas* [fibre sandals]. You can still see the paletos in the old Castilian villages of Spain, where they can spend hours sitting on a bench, their eyes staring into space. Machado, with extraordinary grace and humor, gives us his image of the *paleto* :

> *El paleto perfecto es el que nunca se asombra:*
> *ni aun de su propia estupidez.*
>
> [The perfect rustic is he who is never amazed:
> not even at his own stupidity.][32]

In Machado's juxtaposition of the words *perfecto* and *paleto,* we can hear a faint echo of the Castilian mystical ascesis, the way of perfection. Is Machado hinting that the *via* of this ascesis, this perfection, is through the body, that its goal is our *religare* to those parts in us that have to do with the inert body? Is he pointing to another sort of *via regia* ? If this is so, then he is on the same track as Jung, who says, in his interpretation of the Kundalini Yoga, that its movement for Western man is *down* through the body.[33]

32. Antonio Machado, in *Obras Completas* (Madrid: Editorial Penitud), "Juan de Mairena," p. 1153. For English translation see Ben Belitt (Berkeley: University of California Press, 1963).
33. Jung, in his seminar on the Interpretation of the Kundalini Yoga, makes it clear that the Kundalini Yoga can be useful for Westerners if the movement is downward, a reverse of the upward movement conceived for the Eastern mind. Western man starts out up in Vishuda

If one of the tasks of poetry is to reflect from death, one can imagine that, for Machado, it was important to explore images which, as we have seen in the case of Endymion, have a peculiar connection with death. Machado's image of *el paleto perfecto* – never astonished, just sitting there, gazing into space, not even aware of being a paleto – is a sort of guarantee that one can have insight, poetically, into the part of us which refuses the reflection of death – the Titanic part which chooses, instead, to sleep perpetually with open eyes.

Remember that the Titan Prometheus did not want to reflect from death; he wanted to liberate men from thinking about death: "I caused men no longer to foresee their death," he proclaims in Aeschylus' drama; "I planted firmly in their hearts blind hopefulness."[34] If we have brought together Machado's *el paleto perfecto* and the mythological figure of Endymion, then we are treading on firm ground, since Machado was the poet in whose poetry death was constantly present. He belonged to the tradition of poets who have taught that difficult subject – death. On the subject of death as a 'serious business,' he writes:

Un golpe de ataud en tierra es algo perfectamente serio.

(the throat region, the logos), and so is in need of coming down into those regions of the body alien to him. Jung's insights have to do with the repression of the body in Western Christian culture. My psychotherapeutical conception very much takes into account Jung's vision of this downward movement into the body, the importance of activating the historically repressed body, as well as activating the archetypes of the body – how one imagines one's own body. Jung's interpretation for the Westerner gives a useful background for diagnosing the Westerner's superficial mimetic literal approach to the Kundalini Yoga. Machado, with his poetical image, calls our attention to the body, which Western man finds so difficult to animate. See *Spring 1975,* "Psychological Commentary on Kundalini Yoga," Lectures One and Two – 1932, p. 1; and *Spring 1976,* Lectures Three and Four – 1932, p. 1 (Zürich: Spring Publications).

34. Aeschylus, *Prometheus Bound,* trans. Philip Vellacott (Harmondsworth: Penguin Classics, 1961), p. 28.

[A knock (or rap) of the coffin in the earth is something perfectly serious.][35]

To conclude, a final excerpt from yet another poet. Listen to
how the Endymion complex appeared to him at a random moment in the cave of a modern city, in today's common man:

> Or as, when an underground train, in the tube, stops too long
>   between stations
> And the conversation rises and slowly fades into silence
> And you see behind every face the mental emptiness deepen
> Leaving only the growing terror of nothing to think about.[36]

35. Machado, "En el Entierro de un Amigo," *Obras Completas,* p. 852.
36. T.S. Eliot, "East Coker," III, *Four Quartets,* in *The Complete Poems
    and Plays* (London: Faber and Faber, 1969), p. 180.

CULTURAL ANXIETY

During a discussion once on the problems of Western man, Borges remarked that so-called Western man is not just a Westerner, since we have to take into consideration one particular book in his culture – the Bible – which comes from the East. The Bible is an Eastern product; but no Westerner can avoid the influence of this book and the consequences it has wrought.

The Bible begins with a creation myth.[1] Creation myths can be found in the literature of most cultures, but we have to accept that this Biblical creation myth, which in other cultures would not occupy such a predominant place, gives something special to our culture because it is the basis of what we call our religious belief. Religiously speaking, Western man is a believer; his is a religion of faith. God created man in his own image. This belief has been central to Western man's religious life and, of course, central to containing his psyche and his madness.

As a Western man, living under the historical traditions of my geographical location and race, I feel this Eastern product to be very much a part of me, and I accept that it has a great influence on my life. The essence of the Bible is monotheism: the worship of one God, and the jealousy and wrath of that God if any other is worshiped. This belief has pervaded *in extenso* the world in which we live: our religious belief; our way of life; the ideas of our culture; our politics; the sciences; and, last but not least, the study of psychology. Monotheism is deeply ingrained

---

1. For the psychology of creation myths, see Marie-Louise von Franz, *Patterns of Creativity Mirrored in Creations Myths* (Zürich: Spring Publications, 1972).

in the psychology of every Westerner, no matter what his geography, social condition or education.

Thus, the Bible, the book of monotheism, though geographically alien to Western man, has such a predominant place in his psychology that other books which could be considered to be more truly Western have receded into what we call the unconscious, or are important only to scattered minorities. In fact, the Bible is fundamentally opposed to Western books, an opposition most evident in the books of mythology: the pagan polytheistic books; the books of the many gods and their images; the wealth of the many forms of life. Greek mythology offers the most complete catalogue of images ever produced: forming the stuff of tragedy; the source of poetry and literature; feeding life poetically; peopling the earth with images; building the foundation of philosophy. We must include with the many other mythologies of the Western world: the Northern European mythologies; the hidden tradition and legends of the Celts; the mythologies, legends and poetic conceptions of the autochthonous American peoples, etc. These are the books which have to do with what, in Jungian psychology, we call the collective unconscious.

And then there are the books concerned with the origins of life on earth, the evolution of man, with their provocative discussions about the human race, man's behavior, etc. They are the books which tell us about man's most remote and primitive history, and they make the more humble proposition that humankind is not the crowning achievement of God's creation, but simply another species of animal at a certain level of evolution; this last concept stands in total opposition to the creationism of the Bible.

Western man has written many books during his history: books which actualize the old myths; which tell the story of the history he has lived through; and the great achievement of his literature, in which essential aspects of his psyche are revealed – all of which are the concern of today's psychological studies. Nevertheless, all this wealth at the level of collective consciousness fails to match the Bible – the foreign book from the

East – because the latter has a special effect: it provokes an identification with the text, a collective identification, a power the other books do not have beyond the identification of a small group.

In the Medieval Spanish tradition, there seems to have been an awareness of the identification the Bible provokes. It has never been a book for the masses. In the Church, it has been a book which erudites consulted, and a source of amplification for the saints. Cervantes, in the most important book in Spanish literature, advises us about the madness into which our Lord Don Quixote fell through reading "The Book of Knights" too intensely. I sense in this awareness an old and complex tradition which prevents any literalization of the written word.

Westerners, since the Reformation, have been reading these Eastern Biblical tales, and they have reacted in different ways, ranging from a foolish identification to a tactful or brusque rejection, enabling them to maintain a distance to the book. The point is that the Bible, due to its Eastern ingredient, upsets Western psychology precisely because it triggers off a collective response. It seems the conception of the one all-powerful, imageless God in whom the believer has faith, provokes this kind of psychological identification.[2] And because the Bible provokes identification, it is difficult to talk or write about it psychologically. It is a religious book actuated by faith, and millions of people today identify with it. But it is also the religious book of the Jewish people, the focal point of their life and tradition, and because of its religiosity, there is little or nothing that can be worked out as a psychology. I wonder whether psychology, the individual movement of a psyche, could have anything to do with it. I have always been puzzled by the fact that there have been so many Jewish students of psychology, yet none have done any work on the psychology of Judaism. If

2. I have always thought the Freudian conception of the transference contains the same element as the old Hebrew dependency on an imageless God.

there has been some contribution,[3] it has been very modest, especially if we consider its huge importance for our culture. But perhaps a psychological study of Judaism is impossible; what has been done is more a sort of psychological exegesis of the Bible, or its rather indiscriminate inclusion in studies of comparative religion, down to the amplification method of Jungian psychology.

During the last fifteen years, Jungian studies have paid more attention to monotheism and polytheism, seeing them in terms of polarities that are tremendously relevant to Western man's psyche and to the dynamism of psychotherapy. This is a very different approach from the Jungian amplification method, which distracts the focus from what should be our most urgent concern as Westerners: to differentiate between the monotheism and the polytheism in our Western psyche. Moreover, it is a differentiation to be undertaken with an acute awareness of the historical cultural conflict which exists between these two main streams in the Western psyche. What has been done in this respect has been meager, a rather shy mentioning of the difference between monotheism and polytheism. My intention in this paper is to discuss this issue in terms of a *conflict,* a basic psychological conflict. Further, I consider that it is essential to bring the issue of this conflict out into the open, in order to corner the studies of psychology where they really are (whether people are aware of it or not), where our psyche is most afflicted, an affliction we disguise in the shape of history, religion or politics. It is as if a tabu has been operating in the studies of psychology. Attempts to grasp this basic issue have begun only

3. A relevant contribution to the material of this paper is offered by Rivkah Schärf-Kluger in *Psyche and Bible* (Zürich: Spring Publications, 1974), Part I, p. 3, where she writes: "... one must also take seriously the idea of the chosen people, for it belongs to the main stock of fundamental religious experiences in the Old Testament. The danger of this idea, its 'shadow' so to speak, is hubris, i.e., the danger that the ego of the people, carried by the individuals identified with it, may take possession in an inflationary way of this content that originates in the Self, or may be overwhelmed by it."

relatively recently, so there have been few real repercussions of its implications.

We know that, in the seventeenth century, the foundation of the study of the natural sciences was based, psychologically, on the premise that science had nothing to do with religion. Actually, what gathered together the men of those times to talk about science was precisely that, historically, it had become impossible to express religious differences. Modern science is the child of religious wars full of anxiety, blood and cruelty. The scientific dialogue opened a possible way of relating to each other at a distance from the madness of the major religions. We know also that the cradle of modern psychology was natural science. Even if we presume that the baby is no longer in the cradle, it seems our baby has not grown up enough to be very far from it.[4] It is understandable, therefore, that it has become rather tabu, as I mentioned, to talk about living religion in psychology. I am sure we do not need to be reminded that it was Jung who started to push psychology along the path to religion. But besides these historical complexes, one feels there probably exists some deeper resistance in us which prevents us from viewing our psyche in terms of the polarities of monotheism and polytheism; it is as if, besides the historical complexes which we have inherited, there is an intimate inner tabu, as if the conflict were afflicting our basic nature.

Monotheism and polytheism make up the two basic components in the Western psyche; and we need to be profoundly aware of them both. We need to be more astute at recognizing what emanates from the monotheistic side of life – collective

4. We insist on talking about and discussing psychology with the attitude of the natural sciences, using the same rhetoric, a rhetoric which does not belong to the complexities of psychology. This same way of thinking is applied to the humanities: essays on poetry, for instance, which deal with poetry as if it, too, belonged to the studies of the natural sciences. This makes for tremendous confusion. And, at least in the studies of psychology, what comes out of this confusion, most of the time, is the kind of boring codified jargon which pervades the majority of psychological papers.

consciousness, beliefs, faith (the influence of the Eastern book),
– and what emanates from the more repressed pagan polytheistic side – the archetypal images. But even more important, we
have to become aware of the *conflict,* with its resulting anxiety,
which, from the beginning, these two streams have produced in
the Western soul.

E.R. Dodds, in his *Pagan and Christian in an Age of
Anxiety,*[5] discusses the religious experiences and conflicts during the first centuries of Christianity, calling those times an 'age
of anxiety' after a poetic phrase coined by W.H. Auden. It was
a time when the conflict between traditional paganism and the
new Christian monotheism openly broke out, a time which, in
some ways, can be likened to our own time, which is also an
'age of anxiety.' Dodds' essays, on what for him was historically an age of anxiety, stimulated me into having a wider view
of anxiety and enabled me to see what he says within a more
psychic context. I would say that the Western psyche has always lived with the anxiety produced by the constant conflict
between the pagan mythologies – the many gods with their differentiated images – and the one imageless God of monotheism.
It is an anxiety that arises from a conflict of cultures. There has
always been what I would like to call *cultural anxiety.* Man's
deepest conflicts are cultural, something that psychology cannot
evade.

Dodds' book gives an historical perspective, emphasized by
taking the title of Auden's poem, implying that the feeling of
cultural anxiety is more apparent, more acute, in times of historical extremes. But it is from extremes that reflection begins with
regard to what has always been there and taken for granted.
And here I would like to promote some reflection over this
issue of polytheism and monotheism by pointing out the *obvi-
ousness* of these two sides in the Western psyche. I would then
like to ask a question: Why has it taken psychology so long to
start thinking about the monotheism and polytheism in our-

5. E.R. Dodds, *Pagan and Christian in an Age of Anxiety* (Cambridge:
   Cambridge University Press, 1965).

selves and to realize that these two historical realities form the basis of our conflict? I am aware that this move attempts to reflect the basic standpoint of Jungian psychology from another angle. The study of psychology has been conceived in the dualism of ego consciousness and the unconscious, both being concepts that we might view as imageless cover-ups for the real underlying conflict. Nevertheless, this dualism has been inherited by psychology: one way and only one way of looking into psyche.

What, in fact, we have inherited is a monotheistic bias. It is as if a cameraman were shooting a film with a lens that focuses only on the vertical perspective of ego consciousness and the unconscious. But one wonders, whether what comes out in the film, once the film is developed, consists inevitably of concepts and symbols, not images.[6] I would say, the ego/unconscious

---

6. The structure of the studies of psychiatry and psychology has tended to be based on concepts derived from empirical clinical observations of mental illness. From the beginning of the century, the symbol appeared as dominant in the studies of the unconscious. Freud evidently arrived at his use of symbol, understood by Jung as mere sign and symptom (semiotic), from his studies of conversion hysteria at the turn of the century; on the other hand, Jung began his work as a psychiatrist with psychotic patients, in which he made his great discovery of the religious symbol in the unconscious of those patients. Here the word symbol is appropriately applied, because the original *symbolon* means the union of something previously divided; and symbolism is at the base of most of Jung's ideas on the opposites and the reconciliation of the opposites. In *Psychological Types,* I sense that Jung used symbol and image in an undifferentiated way, giving to them the same value. Later, he became more specific and clearer concerning archetypal images. Images began to be more differentiated, and so provide us, today, with a wider field for exploration, where I consider the more relevant psychological work is going on, and where the symbol is taken as an attribute of the image. A psychotherapy of the image offers a new perspective to hysteria; in the case of psychosis, we sense that the imaginary response to the patient's unconscious symbolism propitiates a better therapy; and a new finding of the image in psychosomatic ailments brings an entirely new approach to the psychotherapy of these complaints.

dichotomy conceptualizes and symbolizes what arises from the unconscious. Whatever conception we have concerning the ego, it is impossible for me to imagine the ego as the receptor of images. Traditionally, it is the soul that receives images; and this is valid for psychic processes and psychotherapy. Now I would like to propose that, without burning the old films, we change the lense of the camera. Then, when shooting our film, we can catch with a sharper focus what comes out of the Judaic monotheistic side of the psyche and what comes out of the pagan polytheistic side, for then it follows that we can begin to differentiate and form a clearer picture of the individual psyche, situated between the two poles, and suffering the anxiety engendered by the conflict. But for this to happen, we have to be particularly aware of what the monotheism in us is doing while we are busy focusing on the polytheism, because our monotheistic ego lense is so automatic.

The change from an ego point of view to having an awareness that embraces both monotheism and polytheism is, for me, of immense importance. And it is a change of view which can only be reached through awareness. In his *Re-Visioning Psychology,* James Hillman says that the last works on Judaic monotheism were by Freud in *Moses and Monotheism,* and by Jung in *Answer to Job.*[7] When discussing this, Hillman somehow transmits a feeling of boredom, implying that the Judaic source has been exhausted and that now the exploration has moved into pagan polytheism. Now to follow this shift is one thing, as it is undoubtedly where the treasury of images is stored, and where the scholarly aspect of psychology has moved. But we must not confuse the scholarly work, fine instrument though it is, with the aim of the study of psyche which, to my mind, would be to catch the psychic conflict.

For we can do a lot of research into the pagan myths and remain unaware of the cultural anxiety generated by the powerful forces of monotheism and polytheism in the psyche. We can

7. James Hillman, *Re-Visioning Psychology* (New York: Harper Colophon Books, 1977), p. 226.

do a lot of research comfortably insulated by our monotheistic bias and repeat what one inheritor of the studies of natural science – Freud – did when, due to his monotheism, he picked out a single polytheistic myth – the Oedipus myth – and made it the original cause of neurosis. He remained unaware that that polytheistic myth has in itself an endless polytheistic imagination to deal with that myth, an imagination very remote from his monotheistic and scientific standpoint.

Personally, I find it difficult to view the psyche in terms of an ego/unconscious opposition. It seems to me particularly unpsychological and belongs to the inheritance from the monotheistic tradition of the ego's identification with monotheism, and thus the repression of what is *not* monotheism. The other perspective I am proposing – the retention of an awareness of both monotheism and polytheism – seems to me more fitting for the study and discussion of psychic processes and for psychotherapy. At least I find myself more at ease with this standpoint. Sometimes one wonders whether the word 'psychology' has been rightly applied to the studies which carry that name. We have to realize that to study psyche from an ego point of view is more absurd than we think.

So let me explain my point of view on this a little further: If instead of remaining in the ego, we embrace the psyche's point of view, we can become more aware of our monotheism and more able to detect when it is operating. Obviously, we cannot have this awareness as long as we remain in the ego, for the ego inevitably carries the monotheistic point of view. We need to recognize the monotheistic rhetoric, to read the monotheistic discourse. We are far too prone to take the monotheistic side for granted. As I said, it is what contributes to a great deal of the cultural anxiety we experience. We cannot go on speculating about psyche, longing to 'make soul,' without having an appreciation of the complexities and ramifications of monotheism in our psyche and our life.

For the analyst who might be interested in becoming aware of both monotheism and polytheism, the challenge would be to learn how to become more acquainted with the difference between the monotheistic and the polytheistic rhetorics: to build up as abundant a memory as possible of their different styles. What for the Renaissance man was the achievement of a 'unified memory,'[8] for the modern analyst might be a differentiation, by way of its rhetoric, of the material emanating from the strong monotheistic side of the culture and of that emanating from the more repressed pagan side. From the viewpoint of psychology today, the Renaissance man's achievement would be of no use to modern man, because there would be no basic differentiation of his cultural anxiety. The art of psychotherapy would be to reflect to the patient from the kind of memory that can at the same time memorize and differentiate between monotheism and polytheism, and, by bringing an awareness of the conflict, break through the patient's cultural anxiety.

If we shift from identification with the ego point of view and move toward a differentiation of monotheism and polytheism in the psyche, we can begin to have an idea of how *guilt,* which in our culture manifests in terms of a strong identification, can now, thanks to a new psychological distance, be insighted as a rhetoric. Guilt, with its endless variations and its embroidery of guilt-making, can be approached as one of monotheism's basic rhetorics, its most obvious one. One can almost say that monotheism can be equated with guilt. The weight of guilt carried by Christianity comes from its dominant Judaic side, from the religious identification in the Jewish tradition (anxiety over keeping within the laws of the religion): "In the beginning was guilt." We know that, in Greek paganism, guilt was not at all important. I remain with Nilsson, who pointed out that it was fundamentally alien to the Greek spirit.[9] When guilt did make

---

8. This is a reference to Giulio Camillo's notion of unifying memory, a memory comprised of the Judeo Christian tradition and the rediscovery of the pagan images, which expressed the longing of the Renaissance man to cope with his cultural anxiety. See Frances Yates, *The Art of Memory* (London: Routledge and Kegan Paul, 1966), p. 155.

9. Martin P. Nilsson, *A History of Greek Religion,* trans. F.J. Fielden (Oxford: Clarendon Press, 1949), p. 217.

an appearance, it was reduced to certain sects – the virginal and puritanical Pythagorean and Orphic sects. Guilt was a sectarian business – anxiety over keeping the rules of the sect. But it was never swallowed by the Greeks in general, and ideas of guilt were rejected.

In all its variations, Western culture is an unconsciously guilt-ridden culture and, inevitably, our psychology has a strong guilt-ridden aspect. In our lives, we can detect the complexities of guilt operating autonomously. We all know people who are successful, refined and cultured, and yet conversation with them on any subject becomes dominated by guilt. There are people who manage to see the events of their life only within the spectrum of guilt, who are skilled at keeping guilt in the foreground, either in themselves or in others, and are unable to conceive of life as anything else than deeply pervaded by guilt. An entire life can become paralyzed by guilt projections upon seemingly banal events: the paralysis of a life rotating systematically around guilt.

As a psychotherapist, one is accustomed to hearing what are often bizarre projections of guilt. If one listens to this kind of autonomous guilt-making from a certain distance and without being caught by that same guilt, if one is detached enough to avoid making a judgment, what one hears is a rhetoric of the absurd. So to approach guilt in terms of a rhetoric is immensely valuable, because it is only through discerning the rhetoric of guilt as an absurdity and an inflation that some degree of awareness occurs. I see guilt as a tremendous inflation, therefore awareness by its very nature is a deflation of guilt. I realize that this proposition of mine to treat guilt as a rhetoric is not an easy one to accept; even I have some difficulty with it. Personally, guilt bores me to death, and I am constantly aware of its psychological uselessness. If it is the image that really moves the psyche, the reading of the psychic image, then I cannot believe that it is possible to read that image in a guilt-ridden state. The image invariably becomes distorted by a feeling which does not belong to it.

We cannot avoid the conclusion that cultural anxiety enters

psychotherapy exacerbated by a host of all-pervading autonomous feelings of guilt. Monotheistic speech is invariably guilt-ridden and, of course, guilt-making, and is in psychic opposition to the endless variety of the archetypal consistent images. Monotheistic guilt is imageless, as is the one God, the source of guilt in our Western culture. For the analyst who accepts cultural anxiety – the conflict between monotheism and polytheism in the psyche – the task is the painful one of learning to discriminate between the rhetorics: the conceptual imageless rhetoric of monotheism and the imaginative rhetoric of polytheism, to withstand the conflict between the two, and to reflect on and value the difference between them.

James Joyce was a great example of a life lived under the pressure of cultural anxiety; in his case, the friction of it generated an energy which transformed it into art. *Ulysses,* that *tour-de-force* of Western literature, expresses what I have been trying to convey about cultural anxiety: the hero, the modern Ulysses, is, paradoxically, a Jew married to an Irish Catholic woman. The guilt-ridden Jesuitical Catholicism and the different kinds of paganisms – the Mediterranean and the author's own Irish Celtic – are the sources of the book's complexities. It is a great work revealing the fragmentation and the madness of the cultural anxiety in the soul of a genius who was able to transform that anxiety into a religious syncretism. With reference to Bloom, W.B. Stanford wrote: "Originally a Jew, then vaguely Protestant and Catholic in turn, Bloom is now an agnostic humanist."[10]

Ulysses is comparable to another *tour-de-force* of religious syncretism (at its best, cultural anxiety is transformed into religious syncretism): Jung's alchemical opus, in which his cultural anxiety was worked out and insighted through Medieval alchemical material. For me, Medieval alchemy was an expression of cultural anxiety, a religious syncretism contained in the alchemical vessel. Jung's cultural anxiety, the con-fusion of the two main sources – the Judaic and the Mediterranean pagan –

10. W.B. Stanford, *The Ulysses Theme* (Oxford: Blackwell, 1968), p. 213.

was worked on in the alchemical retort in a soul which was able
to contain that confusion being based, at a deeper level, in a
Swiss, Celtic, Roman, Germanic paganism.

The involvement of Jung's cultural anxiety can be felt when
he quotes Paracelsus, who said: "… I write like a Pagan though
I am a Christian,"[11] an observation which describes the anxiety
of many men throughout Western history. According to Jung,
the psychic position of being more pagan than Christian contains a feeling of inferiority. It is the position of one who is living from and for the soul, a soul that makes no concessions, no
explanations, no conceptualizations – like that of Joyce or Jung.
I guess Jung himself had this feeling of inferiority to which he,
at times, alluded. He transmits it in his desire to have no followers; his avoidance of falling into criticism; his respect for
other people's complexes; his connection to the other person as
the person was. He never entered the inflation of considering
himself a leader. The resistance he felt against founding the
Jung Institute is well known. One senses Jung's anxiety in his
conflict with the scientific world, so alien to his pagan soul. The
notion of Paracelsus concerning each person with his or her
own star finds an echo in Jung's major concern: individuation.

Joyce and Jung, who happened to be acquainted, both suf-
fered and made their different *opi* under the extreme pressure of
what I like to call cultural anxiety. Both had the strange stamina
given by the mysterious ingredient of the old European Celt,
and both reveal to modern man the main complexities of the
cultural anxiety he lives.

Whereas Joyce and Jung are examples of men who lived
towards the pagan end of the spectrum of cultural anxiety,
Sigmund Freud is an example of a man who lived at the
extreme monotheistic end. He was a child of the Old Testament,

---

11. *CW* 13, para. 148. I recommend a reading of Jung's "Paracelsus as a
    Spiritual Phenomenon" to gain insight into the double cultural anxiety
    lived in the 16th century: on the one hand, the schism in Christianity
    itself and, on the other, the Judaic pagan conflict, expressed by
    Paracelsus as *Pagoyum,* which was one of his favorite neologisms,
    compounded of *paganum* and the Hebrew word *goyim.*

of the Chosen People, that literalization which leads to fantasies
of racial purity. He was also a child of the natural sciences, and
thus under the spell of the search for scientific truth. He has left
us the image of a founder and leader of a school, with followers
who had to accept the scientific psychological discoveries of the
leader as dogmatic truth. Instead of each person having his own
star, he imposed on his followers the monotheistic notion of one
star for everybody. This, in itself, gives us a view of a monotheistic psychology, a psychology which rejects what does not
fit into its monotheistic conception.

Nevertheless, though he occupied that extreme monotheistic
end of the spectrum, it is striking that the elements Freud chose
for expressing his research into psychology were taken from the
pagan polytheistic side of the psyche: the Oedipus complex; the
polymorphous perverse child; Eros and Thanatos, etc. In choosing a polytheistic pagan myth as the basis for his theories, Freud
revealed his own cultural anxiety, and this gives us an impression of the conflict between monotheism and polytheism in in a
predominantly monotheistic mind. His opus is a product of cultural anxiety, too, showing the historical and cultural abyss
between his monotheistic position and the polytheistic sources
he was dealing with. We can appreciate the effort and drama
experienced by a man ostensibly in a position of monotheistic
superiority, trying to deal with pagan inferiorities and feeling all
the discomfort of such a position. One cannot but be moved by
the stamina required for such a task.

However, it is beyond doubt that Freud was not sufficiently
aware of what was going on below the surface of the time in
which he was living. He was blind to the forces gathering in the
unconscious of the people among whom he lived. He was, perhaps, not immune to that strong Jewish fantasy, in the Germanic
countries, of assimilation, an odd fantasy in that it did not take
into account the dilemma of becoming assimilated while remaining the Chosen People. It is impossible for me to equate
social assimilation with religious syncretism. Religious syncretism moves internally; it it a product of cultural anxiety and a
historical and psychic mover. Assimilation at the racial and

social level always remains a collective political problem.

By pointing to these three men whose opi were born of cultural anxiety, I have been trying to show its creative aspect. Now, let us take a look at the other side of the coin; when, out of deep unconscious roots, it erupted into devastating collective madness and destruction. Let us turn to the history of the Jewish people in Germany at the time of National Socialism and the Second World War. Fortunately, in this respect, we are the inheritors of Jung's "Essays on Contemporary Events,"[12] essays that lead the way to the study of collective madness; so to tackle a delicate issue of this sort is well within the Jungian tradition. Jung left no dogma concerning these events; he said they should be reflected from many different angles. Therefore, I believe it will never be out of line to discuss the Holocaust, either in the context of Jung's essays or with a more secret interest motivated by the fears which have grown in us all since Jung left the world.

We must learn again and again from the inexhaustible past, from its complexities that can never be reduced. For, if we can learn from the past, then there is a chance of enriching our present consciousness and maybe even our future. In saying we, I am referring to all Jungians today, while in no way thinking that what we learn can pervade the world. The difference between Jung's generation and our own is that they believed psychology could influence collective events, and we can detect some inflation in that pretension. In any case, we have learned from Jung's "Essays on Contemporary Events," and we can learn still more from them. So let me offer my own personal reading of three of these essays within the framework of cultural anxiety.

The first essay, "Wotan," is a masterpiece on collective psychosis, demonstrating how an archaic Northern European mythological figure took over the German consciousness. In Jungian psychology, this phenomenon is termed possession, or psychosis. But when we study a psychosis, something we are accustomed to doing, we are in fact studying the conflicts which

12. *CW* 10, Part III.

provoked the psychosis. Wotan is an elusive figure, appearing only when the times are propitious and then vanishing again. Jung refers to a monograph on Wotan by Martin Ninck, who, writes Jung, "... describes him ... as the berserker, the god of storm, the wanderer, the warrior ... the lord of the dead ... the master of secret knowledge, the magician ... [Ninck] assumes an inner affinity between Wotan and Kronos, and the latter's defeat may perhaps be a sign that the Wotan-archetype was once overcome and split up in prehistoric times [like Kronos] ... At all events, the Germanic god represents a totality on a very primitive level, a psychological condition in which *man's will was almost identical with the god's and entirely at his mercy.*"[13]

This connection between Wotan and Kronos gives us an appreciation of the archaic forces unleashed by Wotan in the German people. Kronos was the father of the Titans, which puts those archaic forces in the mythological realm of the Titans, thereby deepening our sense of Wotan who disappears for millennia and reappears when the times are propitious, as a chronological phenomenon. The existence of Wotan is in Kronos' time; so we can say that this special collective psychosis is Titanic.[14] Jung says that these archaic forces erupted because Christianity was unable to hold the conflict.[15] There was no religious syncretism to catch and hold in its net the forces of the eruption.

In his discussion on Nietzsche, Jung conveys an image of cultural anxiety, by suggesting that Nietzsche's ostensible confusion between Christ and Dionysos was, in reality, Wotan, that "fundamental attribute" of the German psyche, operating in Nietzsche's psyche. Evidently Nietzsche was not keen on German literature, implying that he could not directly explore the

---

13. *Ibid.,* paras. 393, 394 (italics mine).
14. See Chapter I, "Moon Madness – Titanic Love: A Meeting of Pathology and Poetry," for my approach to the psychology of Titanism.
15. *CW* 10, para. 384.

psychological sources existing in his own backyard, so to speak, with the result that his own Germanic complexes fused with his studies of classical philology, his involvement with Dionysos and the monotheistic thorn in the name of Christ the Saviour.

The third picture of cultural anxiety appears in a footnote about Wilhelm Hauer.[16] Jung knew him, and one senses that Jung had rather ambivalent feelings toward him: on the one hand, Hauer was a scholar of Kundalini Yoga, while on the other, he was a Nazi. As the founder and leader of the German Faith Movement, he became possessed with the demented idea of creating a German religion of faith without a Christian element. It was a new and even crazier rejection of the possibilities in historical religious syncretism: the rejection of the monotheistic book from the East, as if this book, which his own Luther had brought to the people, had become an intolerable image. He was proposing a pure *virginal* German religion, uncontaminated by the Judaic Christian influence.

Jung's essay on Wotan is a diagnosis, impeccably worked out, of a collective psychosis, the psychotic condition of the Germans at the time of National Socialism.

In the second essay, "After the Catastrophe," a masterpiece in the study of the psychopathic personality and collective psychopathy, there is no longer even the remote possibility of an image: only anxiety and guilt expressed at the psychopathic level. There is no longer the unconscious dynamism of an archaic figure taking over the situation. After reading "After the Catastrophe" several times, one comes to the conclusion that guilt and psychopathy are so closely linked that you cannot talk about one without the other. I would even go so far as to say that psychopathy equals guilt and guilt equals psychopathy. If we accept this kinship, then it follows that whenever guilt appears, there is, at the least, a psychopathic component. From Jung's reflections in this essay, one gets the impression that the only way to deal with psychopathy is by means of guilt. It seems, when confronted with the psychopath, guilt is invariably

16. *Ibid.,* para. 387, 16n.

present. We put the guilt onto the psychopath, and the psychopath projects the guilt onto someone or something else. Psychopathy is rife with guilt. First, Jung places the guilt for the catastrophe with the Germans – with the psychopaths – but then he goes further and places the guilt with the whole of Europe. We are introduced to the first grand vision of psychopathy: it is part of human nature; we all have a psychopathic part which varies in extent; it is in each person, and can manifest collectively.

It is in this essay that one feels Jung's cultural anxiety as in no other of his papers.[17] One senses it most strongly when he burdens the Germans with guilt, as if guilt is the inevitable language when the psychopath comes to the fore. In my paper on Titanism, I tried to work out guilt as belonging to the imageless part of the psyche, guilt coming from the lacuna where no image is possible. Now, in this present paper, we have discussed guilt as being at the core of the monotheistic imageless God. I consider Jung's "After the Catastrophe" to be a great research into the imageless part of human nature, what I associate with the psychopathic component. However, one feels that Jung, in writing his paper, was at the high point of his own cultural anxiety, when it could no longer be contained and worked upon imaginatively, but was spilling over into anger and guilt. It was a desperation which could only be expressed by way of the language of guilt. Guilt was constellated. Jung is telling us that one of the reactions to psychopathy is anger. He did not place the guilt with the Germans in a manipulative or guilt-making way; he placed it with all the honest anger and rage he was able to express in writing, and he moves us to accept our own anger

---

17. One is deeply moved by Jung's cultural anxiety. When thinking about the wonder of the Renaissance, he said that, had it not been for that little German priest, the Renaissance would have given us the most extraordinary rebirth of ancient culture. But then, in "Wotan," he implies that Protestantism would have been the right Christian answer. All his cultural anxiety is in this contradiction: his dilemma in being caught between Protestantism and Catholicism, not to mention the fainting at the *Hauptbahnhof*; we can faint when in extreme anxiety (Kolb).

and rage as a natural response to psychopathic behavior.

"Fighting with the Shadow," the third essay, has an enticing title. If "Wotan" is about the eruption of a Northern European archaic figure and "After the Catastrophe" is about the horror of the psychopath, then we can only engage in what the third essay is all about: fighting the shadow. It is a precise title, particularly for those of us who learn psychology from the study of the shadow, which, as far as I can see, is the only way to expand psyche and the study of psychology. The fight with the shadow allows us to free ourselves from the strait-jacketed view of Wotan as pure psychosis, and the catastrophe as pure psychopathy. Between the two extremes – psychosis and psychopathy – lies the psychic possibility of fighting the shadow or, at any rate, becoming a little more aware of what we mean by shadow, namely, what we do not know about human nature.

All that psychosis and psychopathy made possible the Second World War with its eighty million casualties, among them six million Jews. But it was the killing of those six million Jews – what is known as the Holocaust – that makes the Second World War quite different. And the Holocaust is central to cultural anxiety because, without the extermination of six million Jews, the other deaths would have been counted as in any other war, the usual kind of war, of generals fighting generals. Furthermore, *viewed from the perspective of cultural anxiety,* the Holocaust can teach us about shadow. The Holocaust is in fact particularly relevant to the subject here under discussion – cultural anxiety – because it was the result of a religious and racial conflict; and relevant also to fighting the shadow, since there was the mad fantasy of destroying a shadow, utterly, because of the impossibility of assimilating it. The Holocaust was a shadow conflict.

So if there was an archetype at work in all the psychosis, psychopathy and horror of the Holocaust, it was the archetype of purity: the virgin.[18] The virgin is an archetype that constel-

18. The original paper, "On Cultural Anxiety," was written as part of a work in progress on Artemis, the archetype of virginity and purity.

lates intolerance and thus casts a dark shadow. Moreover, we can establish an affinity between monotheism and virginity in that they are both exclusive: they do not tolerate any form of life other than their own. There is no doubt that a peculiar affinity exists between monotheism and virginity. (We have only to think of the history of Christianity and the Christian missionaries.) Euripides, the poet of the irrational, reminds us of the bloody butchery that went on in Tauris to find the victims offered to Artemis, presenting us with an image which can be seen as a prototype of massacre: in the sense of offering human sacrifices to the Virgin Goddess of purity. So, without going into the history of the Jewish diaspora in Germany, a subject beyond my scope, in what follows, I believe I can put forward a view of the Holocaust in terms of virginity that is not terribly difficult to accept: the Holocaust as the horrifying result of two peoples driven by the madness of virginal purity. It is this virginal fantasy of two pure races that gives to the Second World War its psychological peculiarity and makes the cruelty of the Holocaust a unique episode in Western history.

But, first, let me make a small digression: One of the most misused terms in this century's psychology is 'aggression'; its abuse is convincing enough. Until recently, the ideas concerning aggression, found in studies of animal behavior, anthropology, etc., were that man has an instinctual aggression like the animals. According to these ideas, what goes wrong in man is that the so-called primitive complexes break out and take over the 'self-controlled, civilized' individual. The blame, with a certain hypocrisy, is projected onto the primitive man we all have in us somewhere. All sorts of theories were elaborated in this connection, even one concerning the old brain and the new brain, the new brain being threatened by the old primitive brain. Today, however, the latest books on evolution[19] offer us more sophisticated psychological ideas, more in keeping with the spirit of our times. If man had only an instinctual aggression,

19. For instance, Richard E. Leakey, *The Making of Mankind* (New York: Dutton, 1981).

then it would be contained within the ecology of his instincts. But it is more complex than this. Aggression at the level of so-called primitive man, who knows more or less how to deal with it, falls too short for explaining what we see in the world today.

Throughout recorded history, so-called human aggression would seem to spring from cultural conflicts, an expression of man's cultural anxiety; and if the recent books on evolution present primitive aggression as being more than just instinctual, as being a product of culture, then there is nothing to compare with today's so-called civilized man, applied to whom the word aggressive is no longer valid. It is a word out of context and simply not strong enough. As aggression is lived at the more primitive level, for the civilized man with his excess of cultural conflict, I prefer to use the word cruelty.

In accepting the Jungian term of shadow as the field for exploration, depth psychology must include cruelty, a by-product of culture and civilization, as an essential component of shadow. I think of cruelty as being within the human possibility of fighting the shadow, as something accessible enough to remain within our daily awareness: cruelty is cultural, and therein lies its potential to become psychic It is as if history were constantly modifying our view of this issue. We cannot have the same view of this human trait as we had fifty years ago: cruelty increases. Historically speaking, Jung, as well as his followers and collaborators, worked on this part of human nature in terms of evil. They tackled it mostly within the Western religious tradition of the polarities between good and evil, or evil as the part of our nature we cannot deal with and have to reject.

To summarize: Bearing in mind these three facets of human nature, we are trying to differentiate what belongs to the darkest part of our shadow. Aggression is an instinctual attitude appearing in the conflicts of primitive man, and also at the primitive level of the psyche and our complexes. (We could perhaps use the word aggression for some of the attitudes and behavior of children and the mentally ill.) Cruelty is a product of civilized man's cultural anxiety. Of course, aggression and cruelty overlap. And finally, in the studies of Western religion and philosophy, evil remains in the framework of the polarities between good and evil, the latter, in Jungian psychology, being the part of our nature we cannot assimilate and therefore have to reject.

But, for our personal survival, for the protection of our souls, cruelty is the facet on which to concentrate. It is our most immediate concern, an all too evident part of our daily lives, of the world and of our practices, where we are accustomed to seeing cruelty disguised in psychiatric diagnosis and treatment. Cruelty is an element of our constant cultural anxiety. We are all cruel in some respect. The political tortures and murders of today are closer to us than we may care to admit. Indeed, we are far from those Socratic days when, in spite of cruelty, Eros was the main concern. Borges put it very clearly when he said that you can know everything, even be a great poet, but if you do not know about cruelty, you know nothing.

This attempt at a differentiation will not withstand much criticism, but its purpose was to arrive at a part of the psyche where we can perhaps tackle this dark shadow aspect of human nature: to concentrate on cruelty. Moreover, after this digression, I think we have a better perspective from which to view the Holocaust as a shadow conflict; this has little to do with the way in which it has been fundamentally seen in terms of victims and victimizers, but rather that it is a manifestation of cruelty as a by-product of cultural anxiety.

"Being victim seems to be the destiny of Jews,"[20] said a modern Jewess, Golda Meier, to a modern Jew, Henry Kissinger; as if this were the price to be paid for the fantasy of being the Chosen Ones. Her statement implies almost an unconscious longing. There is a strange psychology in this acceptance of being the victim, a psychology of being driven by a destiny that unconsciously precipitates the search for the victimizer. It is a destiny which has an extraordinary strength and the skill to find the portion needed for the living forces of that destiny. If the goal of one's destiny is to become a victim, then all a person's energy goes into that. If the final purpose is to be a victim, then

20. Quoted in *Time Magazine,* February, 1982.

one imagines that this is what really brings fulfillment. Such a sense of destiny turns a life into the vehicle for that driving force. This is how I prefer to view the history of the Jewish diaspora in Germany: the Jewish people, driven by the force of their destiny – their racial purity – down the centuries propitiating and building up to the final consequences of the Holocaust.

Being chosen and being the victim are the same, and being chosen is a paradigm for purity. Let a twentieth-century writer, George Orwell, in his *1984,* written at another time of extreme cultural anxiety, describe the kind of monotheistic rejection which makes the madness of racial purity possible; he was actually concerned with how purity appears in the latest monotheistic conception of life: today's state monotheism:

> What was required in a Party member was an outlook similar to that of the ancient Hebrew who knew, without knowing much else, that all nations other than his own worshipped 'false gods.' He did not need to know that these gods were called Baal, Osiris, Moloch, Ashtaroth, and the like: probably the less he knew about them the better for his orthodoxy. He knew Jehovah and the commandments of Jehovah: he knew, therefore, that all gods with other names or other attributes were false gods.[21]

The shadow, this madness of racial purity, this exclusiveness, cast, in turn, constellated the German madness of racial purity: racial purity constellating racial purity. What history revealed in Germany was the killing of 'pure' Jews by 'pure' Germans: the pure Aryan race versus God's Chosen People. Two virginally dominated conceptions of life, the outcome of which was insanity. The impact of two virginal psychologies resulted in a mass destruction, a massacre. Victims and victimizers, victimizers and victims, dancing together in a hellish ballet of death. Moreover, it was in this demented appearance of virginity that the most destructive element lay, where seemingly the destruction focused, almost as if the whole terrible war were

21. George Orwell, *1984* (Harmondsworth: Penguin, 1981), p. 246.

a mere pretext to make possible the shadow meeting of two racial purities.[22]

We are not accustomed to finding madness in the Jewish conception of their religious and racial purity. But, from the psychological angle, we are obliged to see it as a madness. For, we have been trained to perceive in terms of Jung's equation of religion equalling madness. As a religious people, we feel the way in which religion is a net to catch and contain our madness. But Jung also trained us to see religion as the field of the unconscious, where the shadow lurks, where cultural anxiety is most evident; in other words, the field to study.

In this chapter, I have offered a psychology of the Holocaust which seems to me a more profitable way of studying it at this point in time. It is a psychology well rooted in Jung's legacy of the collective unconscious, the historical complexes and the shadow. I prefer to view the Holocaust in terms of cultural anxiety and the constellation of two shadows, both with their cruelty, than at the level of guilt or that of victims and victimizers.

E.R. Dodds, in *The Greeks and the Irrational,* says, rather convincingly, that when paganism was in decline before Christianity took over as the one ruling religion, the dominant attitude, in the Western soul, was a "fear of freedom.."[23] So the fear of the many was assuaged under the protection of the One. But if, in our own times, we find a parallelism to Dodds' 'age of anxiety' (times which herald big changes in the world), we cannot say that today's soul finds much of a refuge in monotheism: because it is that selfsame monotheism which is producing the fear; which does not respect the right to be different; which has the fantasy of building one monotheistic world. Today, the world is caught in the ultimate terror of the clash between two predominant systems: one, the North American monotheism

---

22. If we read the documents on the war, we come to the conclusion that the Nazi High Command was more obsessed with the Jews than with what was happening on the war fronts.
23. E.R. Dodds, *The Greeks and the Irrational* (Berkeley: University of California Press, 1968), Chapter VIII, "The Fear of Freedom."

conceived from that same mixture of racialism and religion, the white Anglo Saxon Protestants (the WASPS), readers of the Bible (the Eastern book); the other, the monotheistic excess of Russia, the monotheistic conception of the State. In spite of any awareness they might have of each other's shadow, these two monolithic systems seem bent on destroying each other. They both have that dangerous virginal ingredient of purity – the one Biblical, the other ideological – and in their struggle, they produce today's fear. It is an historical situation which touches everyone, notwithstanding their history and geography.

In writing this chapter, I would like to finish by stressing how much I have taken into consideration my own immediate historical complexes.[24] I am a Caribbean man, an historical product of the Caribbean section of what is called the Latin American Baroque. It is a mixture of Christianity in its Spanish version – a rather good balance between a Trinitarian monotheism and the old images rooted in the Mediterranean, plus a strong Celtic component. This is, in itself, a religious syncretism, producing its own anxiety and dynamism. But it is a religious syncretism which made an even wider syncretism possible: the fusion with the many different autochthonous American religions, not forgetting the religions the Africans brought with them in their souls.

In this brief summary of the syncretism called the Latin American Baroque, I do not want to leave out the cruelty of our history – the piracy, the constant tyranny. We are a people who have to put a lot of energy into balancing our cultural anxiety: between the poets and the tyrants, the tortures, the shadow I want to call cruelty. And ours is a brand of cultural anxiety that occupies a wider space in the spectrum spanning monotheism and polytheism. What is more, it obviously leans more toward the polytheistic end and shows that inferiority when seen in relation to the monotheistic end. It is out of these complexities that I feel the fear of monotheism and see it more as a menacing

---

24. In most psychological papers, Jungian analysts tend not to acknowledge openly the historical complexes behind them.

excess than as a challenge to the images in my soul, the images that nourish one's sense of life.

Cultural anxiety is my way of reflecting the inherited historical conflict, in any Westerner's psyche, between monotheism and the many paganisms of the Western world. Cultural anxiety could be seen in many other ways, and I presume each person has his or her own way of accepting and dealing with this anxiety. It is not difficult to think that Jung's concept of the Self was his way of holding the One and the many. But, as a man who has learned from Jung's teaching, I would say, in this respect, that to follow the tracks of one's own individuation is what is really valid. I personally feel that, in the world we live in, tolerance, as a way of understanding, is fundamental. However, I am also aware that inside me there are elements prone to tolerance and elements prone to intolerance; I have to suffer the anxiety these two opposites bring about in me, and I feel the challenge of trying to tolerate what is, in itself, intolerant.

REFLECTIONS ON THE DUENDE

(An examination of *The Theory and Play of the Duende*
by Federico García Lorca)
Dedicated to María Fernanda Pa│

At first sight, the opening lines of García Lorca's essay, *¹*
Theory and Play of the Duende[1] (hereafter referred to as ⸢
Duende) look like an incrimination, but considered at grea│
length, we realize that they are intended as reflections on teac│
ing, culture and the history of culture in our time, something ⸢
vital concern to the life and soul of modern man.

García Lorca begins his talk by recalling how, during his te│
years as a student, he had heard "nearly a thousand lectures" i│
the same elegant salon in which he was then speaking and adds:
"longing for fresh air and sunlight, I was so bored that when I
emerged I felt as if I was covered with a thin film of ash that
was about to turn into itching powder."[2]

His attack was aimed at teaching, at those thousand mean-
ingless lectures which, like Ixion's wheel, could be repeated in
an infinite cycle. A thousand lectures giving us a glimpse of
García Lorca's feeling of irritation that comes through to us as a
curse of titanic and hellish dimensions. A thousand lectures
which at best provide a plethora of information that can never
be fully assimilated or experienced, and in practice exists to
deepen the abyss between knowledge and that which knows
within us: the soul.

1. Federico García Lorca, *Obras Completas* (Madrid: Editorial Aguilar.
   XIII Edc., 1967).
2. Federico García Lorca, *Ibid.*, p. 109.

In philosophy and the history of scholarship (in this case, they seem to be combined), Nietzsche was the innovator of his age when it came to stating the problem. On the verge of madness, he wrote that the conflict of present-day man was a very old one. He demonstrated it by way of adolescent intuitions about classical Greece, in such insoluble dichotomies as Apollo and Dionysus. But there is no doubt that he was the first to sound the trumpet and draw attention to that which history had forgotten and pushed out of sight. Nevertheless, we know that this patrimony abandoned millennia ago still exists somewhere in our being. We know that it is there by "disorderly" outbursts, pathology and suffering in their most immediate forms, by misunderstandings, by the effort it costs us to come anywhere near understanding things that have no frame of reference in the life that history has forced upon us. We know it, too, because sometimes we experience these long forgotten feelings as a means of access to our innermost being ... when our emotions are stirred, when a few glasses of wine, good company, the lines of a poem or the rhythmic melody of music, or even a dream, move something within us.

Philosophy could not accept the challenge and make the effort to offer new answers. Instead, it followed other paths, those of the thousand lectures with the attendant exploration of linguistic intricacies, the assertions of science increasing the boundless greed of the titanic and the deification of the economy. Finally, when it came to exploring man, it revealed to us the existential vacuum already found in literature, the void where the Duende can never appear. Scholars did indeed accept the challenge and sensed something that was already in the atmosphere, a kind of need for the man of this century to breathe more deeply, but an "inspiration" that would be like absorbing air, stimuli and images from far beyond the limits of the air which normally reaches our lungs. For what can best sustain our needs has to find its way from the remote regions bypassed by history; what is most precious comes from there – the body.

The initiators of these studies focused our attention on a

central geographic problem. They were humanists who lived north of the Alps, Germans steeped in a tradition for which Dionysus had no meaning as a theme until the second half of the 19th century. Moreover, when historical necessity forced them to study it, they did so with the very tools provided by the history of humanistic studies in which they were trained. By this, I mean the historical, racial and geographical considerations which today we call Transalpine psychology, though they themselves were not aware that this was the psychic background of their own studies. They were the children and grandchildren of a Protestantism imbued with fantasies of imperialistic dominion which distanced them from positions more favorable to the personal inner experience of what they were studying. Euphoric and steeped in an incurable optimism, they began to explore the irrational from the incubator of Nazi shame, from that other (Wotanic) madness which bore no relation to the one they were studying. In all events, through the romantic agonies of their souls, they handed down to us an erudite tradition and some of them the extremely valuable expression of their limitations. As Walter Otto puts it: "Thus previous attempts to explain the madness of the Dionysian orgies in terms of human needs, whether spiritual or material, have ended in complete failure. Their conclusions are not only unbelievable in themselves, but they are intolerably contradictory of the most important and the most explicit sources."[3]

These lines tell us clearly how remote these scholars were from the irrational Dionysian complexes, where the incredible and the rejected manifest themselves in a single body, in as much as contradictions are an inherent and essential feature of Dionysus. Otto's words also indicate the boundary lines between academic studies of the humanities and something that eludes them, the territory of the subterranean gods where study, whatever we mean by the word, reaches its limits and lived experience begins. We cannot conceive of Dionysus as belief.

3. Walter Otto, *Dionysus, Myth and Cult.* (Indiana University Press, 1965), p. 133.

He is living experience: emotions, feelings, complaints, cries of grief and bodily expressions: manifestations through which lives repressed by consensus and relegated to the social and geographical sidelines in their constant battle for survival made their attempts at self-expression. I speak of those defeated by history, as was the case with García Lorca's Duende which lives on in Andalusia, a region steeped in its Roman, Jewish, Moorish and Gypsy complexes.

Since the turn of the century, other disciplines have tried to tackle the problem. One approach is psychotherapy, the psychic process reflected and accepted as life. Here I should point out that this is a personal point of view that is central to my studies. Psychotherapy cannot dispense with scholarship (the study of culture), the source from which it draws its nourishment. What in scholarship remained mere love of study is carried into life by the talking cure, thus complementing what the last century gave us in its study of culture.[4]

Psychotherapy can initiate processes and healing, always providing we admit that the sick person is the product of a particular history and culture. Thus, a psychotherapy not founded on culture, or a psychotherapist who does not have a cultured view of life and is unaware that sickness has its roots in cultural complexes, is inconceivable. Once we realize that illness is essentially repression, the repression of gods or goddesses, psychotherapy's chief concern then becomes observation and evaluation of the appearance of the gods who favor the reflection of psychic elements, gods whose epiphanies evince a world and life of their own. In our culture, the pagan gods and the forms of life they personify are the most repressed; that is why they are the very gods who trigger our deepest psychic movements.

In talking about repression, I want to rise to a higher cultural level, rejecting the jargon of the age which maundered on about the "repressive" and placed itself outside the historical and religious complexes of civilized life by concentrating exclusively

4. Pedro Laín Entralgo, *The Therapy of the Word in Classical Antiquity*, trans. L.J. Rather and John M. Sharp, (Yale Univ. Press, 1970).

on the personal aspect. A psychotherapy focused on personal systems cannot even approach, much less penetrate, the complexities of a culture. But having said that, the clinic for the mentally ill, the psychotherapist's consulting room and the study of psychosomatic processes may well be understood as observations of the actual world which can, I feel, at times grant us a vision of the irrational as it emerges, leaping over the barriers of repression and trying desperately to come alive.

The total boredom induced by these thousand lectures inspires García Lorca to propose a different, more stimulating knowledge and one more in keeping with the demands of psychotherapy and the studies of modern scholarship. Here I speak specifically and exclusively about a psychotherapy linked to study of the archetypes, where apprenticeship to the psyche begins and becomes possible; where the study of the irrational needs to be seen from within the archetypal forms and limits to which it belongs.

Study of the irrational has already become much more accessible in this part of the century, as numerous contributions on the subject demonstrate. It seems as if scholars were closer to the irrational[5]; as if from the viewpoint of the age in which they were destined to live and study they had come closer to the realm from which Lorca transmits his Duende to us. It also seems as if scholars, driven by historical necessity, have gone more deeply into the interrelationship of theory and play proposed by Lorca: theory and play, to be sure, but a theorizing with all its implications, including the erudite associations and intellectual connections Lorca offers us, much in the manner of his time, rounded off with his special brand of surrealist wit and charm. The Duende has its forms.

But let us leave all this within the theoretical framework of the scholars and we shall see that the addition of *play* urges us to embark on deeper, more favorable relations with those theories. This brings us to the consideration of an impressive book

5. So much so that the latest contributions to the theme of Greek tragedy look upon emotions as the first subject to be dealt with.

on classical Greek themes by E.R. Dodd entitled *The Greeks and the Irrational*,[6] a splendid contribution to scholarship. The autobiography of the author,[7] an Irish scholar, also recounted the games with the irrational it was his lot to experience. They included the madness of a world engrossed in political and social conflicts, the psychology of those defeated by historical complexes, by what can never be resolved, and his friendship with great poets (always of capital importance), whose work owes so much to the irrationality of divine intervention, cannabis, parapsychological societies and dreams.

With the publication of E.R. Dodds' valuable work on the irrational, we have the impression that the fields of psychology and culture are drawing closer, becoming more accessible and that scholars are approaching the irrational more intuitively, indirectly giving us backing and taking us even closer to Andalusia, the corner of the world from which García Lorca bequeathed us his masterly essay on the *Theory and Play of the Duende*.

Here we shall confine ourselves to seeing the possible fusion of the *daimon* as an immanence with a personal accent and language which comes to us through intuitions. By this I mean something instinctive which appears arbitrarily at times and may even emanate from the so-called absurd and the divine intervention of a god. That is as far as we dare to tread. It would be irreverent to take one step further into the precincts of the mystery because that might be the setting for the epiphany of a god, in that differentiated element of individuation which speaks to us from the unfathomable and which we call *daimon*. And Lorca, full of Andalusian joy, tells us that the Duende is none other than the descendent of the lively demon of Socrates. Fusion takes place in a state of confusion, and the moments of the 'happening' are lived in confusion. Thus, an attempt to go

---

6. E.R. Dodds, *The Greeks and the Irrational* (Berkeley: Univ. of California Press, 1968).

7. E.R. Dodds, *Missing Persons, An Autobiography* (Oxford: Clarendon Press, 1978).

further with the Duende from where Lorca left it – such a necessity of the age, the transformative substance of that which belongs to psyche and psychotherapy – would not only propitiate today's vital interest in the field of classical studies, but make our own studies more worthwhile.

I want to take Lorca's essay as a text, but one with a more vital content than that which scholars have accustomed us to since the second half of the 19th century, although I should point out that today their material has a more appropriate, deeper vision, with historical pressures and interests that transcend the confines of academe. If Lorca's essay is a text, its importance will be enhanced if we realize that the subject of most of the profoundly boring thousand lectures that he attacked was creativity, which means that they lend themselves to speculations and digressions whose subjectivity is neither divine nor daimonic: they are simply puerile attempts to prophesy creative genius: promising IQ's, hysterias accepted as divine revelations. It is a creativity conceived in titanic sweat, revolving endlessly like the notorious thousand lectures, and most of it leads to unrecognized exhaustion or irremediable breakdowns. Consequently, if our task today is to teach, to educate with soul, creativity is tantamount to creating soul. Now Lorca's essay has become a text, a source of reference introducing us to new studies, while suggesting that we study the same works, approaching them, however, with a different vision, a vision that is within us and has been veiled for thousands of years. To reach that corner of Andalusia, García Lorca's environment, and to be fortunate enough to sense the Duende is like going to a "reservoir" of ancient Mediterranean initiation, ceremonies where the Duende as initiation is conjured up step by step in a ritual that cannot be learned.

So we see that the appearance of the Duende is *studied,* propitiated and expected in Andalusia. Thus we now have books like *El Arte del Flamenco,*[8] a book which is unusual because it

---

8. D.E. Pohren, *El Arte del Flamenco* (Sevilla, España: Sociedad de Estudios Españoles, Finca Espartero).

was written by D.E. Pophrens, born in Minneapolis, Minnesota, who received the 1970 National Prize awarded by the Chair of Flamencology at Jerez de la Frontera; or we can also read Don Luis Bollain, authority on matters taurine, who writes about the century's bullfighting and who told me about the bullfighting courses given at the University of Seville during the winter terms. Thus, we find that two men of widely different origins, one an American, the other a dyed-in-the-wool Spaniard, are both explorers of the Duende, whose treatises, by dint of "stubborn repetition," as Don Luis puts it, open us to the kind of teaching and education which would give access to the possibility of the Duende's appearance. This leads us to say that flamenco and bullfighting are *studied* as an exercise which teaches and prepares us to recognize and withstand the appearance of the Duende within us. In other words, to cultivate our own sensibility to the Duende. What is the Duende if not that very special moment of truth when the soul and a god who appears in his own field are fused in confusion, both in flamenco choruses and bullfighting, reaching the *daimon* in each one of us? Here we have individuality and the collective in fusion. This alters the concepts of individuation, seeing that the Duende is a highly "individuated" product which is experienced in its own emotion, making us feel our inwardness, though it is simultaneously manifested in a collective framework. Flamencology and the art of bullfighting are treatises on how to gain access.

Lorca says that in bullfighting the Duende appears in the opening *veronicas* when the bull is still intact or in the final act, when the matador moves in for the kill. In Lorca's day, the Mad Twenties of bullfighting, there were great artists in killing in the manner of *volapié* – bullfighters who took a delight in it. A public on tenterhooks watched the bullfighter preparing the bull for the supreme thrust. In those days, a perfect *volapié* was still the most highly prized way of killing. Nowadays it is out of fashion, but this does not mean that one day it will not come back into its own. For the matador to profile himself, hurl himself at the bull from exactly the right distance, with his eyes fixed on the *morillo,* perform the crossover, thrust his sword in and come out cleanly, slowly, by the bull's flanks, with the horns only inches from his body, is something that defies any imaginable conception of time and space. This is living art, a reenactment of the primordial image of the bull's death, the primordial mass. Perhaps one day this ritual may reappear in its essential perfection so that, as Don Luis says, we may see with our own eyes the sword entering the bull's neck in exactly the right spot with astounding slowness and the Duende making his appearance there. But we all feel that the bull's death in the ring goes far beyond the virtuosity that a good matador may display at a particular moment. When some bulls die in the ring, in that moment of agony between the final sword thrust and death, time seems to stand still and a *temple* is created, a space which stirs our senses, because – why not say it? – there are bulls that die magnificently, as if giving a lesson in dying to everyone in the bullring.

As I have already said, today it is difficult, if not impossible, for the Duende to appear during the final sword thrust. However, to give the reader some idea of what I mean, I refer him to the commentaries of the great bullfighting authority, Don José María de Cossío, in his famous encyclopedia, *Los Toros*.[9] Writing about Diego Mazquirará 'Fortuna,' a great artist of *volapié* in Lorca's day, he says: "Without a doubt, Diego Mazquiarán 'Fortuna' is one of the greatest matadors ever recorded, or who ever will be recorded in the history of bullfighting. Possibly he was the best of his day, which coincided with the glorious period of the two colossi, Joselito and Belmonte, or at least with the best and most important part of that period. 'Fortuna' was a stylist, a virtuoso of the *volapié* kill. He dominated and executed the *suerte* to perfection. There was no one to compare with him in the way he observed the *tiempos* of the act. When entering to kill, he took up his position at the distance required by the qualities of the bull, an undeniable exhibition of his perfect understanding of the *suerte,*

9. José María Cossío, *Los Toros* (Madrid: Sexta Edic., Espasa-Calpe, 1969).

whereas many matadors of star billing had the defect of always placing themselves at the same (long or short) distance from the bull at the supreme moment. All this, and his personal presence, gave an unsurpassable beauty and arrogance to the act and motivated the delirious ovations that were lavished on him."[10]

We can take the moment when the bullfighter enters to kill as a propitious frame of reference for the appearance of the Duende. As I have already mentioned, this moment has all but disappeared nowadays, but what remains a possibility is the appearance of the Duende in the bullfight at the other moment mentioned by Lorca. José Luis Vázquez, son of the matador of the same name, made his first appearance as a *novillero* in the Plaza de las Ventas in Madrid on September 9, 1979. He used the cape on his first bull and gave it six-and-a-half *veronicas.* Suddenly I shot to my feet; my face was bathed in tears and then, like a spring, I recoiled, feeling I know not what. I don't remember if I shouted: what I do know is that when I turned around, everyone in the crowd seemed to share my delirium. All around me, old *aficionados* gave way to the same frenzy, their faces covered with tears. The Duende had made his appearance in a series of *veronicas* which defied description. The next day, a journalist reported what an old *aficionado* had told him: "Those veronicas made me feel twenty years younger." Here the Duende, as if pointing to a rebirth, catches us from below we know not where, and in touching dormant essences is felt as a rebirth, a reaffirmation of life.[11]

But let us say a few more words about bullfighting; let us try to approach the mystery which makes the appearance of the Duende in the bullfight possible, referring to Don Luis Bollain

10. José María de Cossío, *Ibid.,* Vol. III, p. 575.
11. The reader should not think that my reading of the scholars is literal or direct. I mentioned this on the first page of my book, *Hermes and His Children.* Until recently, Death and Resurrection were associated with tragedy, with ritual, with the cycle of the year and the vegetation rites forming its origins. As far as I am concerned, the psychical element of the experience of death and rebirth refers entirely to the emotional side.

and his treatise, *El Toreo,* and reduce a whole book devoted to the essence and aesthetics of tauromachy to the conception of the *temple.* "I understand *templar* as meaning to harmonize, attune and impart the same rhythm to the movement of the lure (the cape or *muleta* held by the bullfighter) and the charge of the bull so that the bull always has the cloth within reach, but never manages to reach it."[12] A difficult art, infinitely more complicated than can be imagined from the lines quoted here, and a dynamic essence propitious to the Duende's appearance.

I should like to expand on the concepts and intuitions that other writers have expressed when trying to describe the *temple.* *Temple* is slowness, but that does not mean that it is uniquely and exclusively slow. I prefer to describe it as an enormously animated slowness, a slowed down state of being, the psyche being adequately prepared. *Temple* is a slowness of movement that may appear in some bullfighting *suertes,* in singing or dancing flamenco and – why not say it? – in life itself: it pertains to its essence. We can also feel it at times when we are listening to essentially Dionysian music, when the jazz or blues singer or black spiritual choirs sing in those dark sounds to which Lorca refers and with a *temple* matching the tempo they require to transmit their emotion and their Duende. *Temple* is the central nerve and its appearance in psychotherapy points to Dionysian constellations, tells us clearly about the psychic element of inner movement and about the classical constellation of the Dionysian body, even more so if we know and accept that tradition has assimilated Dionysus and his wife Ariadne to the couple Eros and Psyche. Thus, when there are a few seconds of *temple* between patient and psychotherapist during treatment, they are more nourishing, more important and say more to the psyche than the hours of reductive interpretations, inflationary amplifications and endless associations. Genuine *aficionados* already know this: especially the small minority that goes to the bullring to see if the miracle of those ineffable seconds will

12. Luis Bollain, *El Toreo* (Sevilla: Católica Española, S.A., 1968), p. 173.

appear. Moreover, when referring to it, the metaphor they use is the symbolic attribute closest to the Psyche (the flask of perfume). This kind of bullfighting *aficionado* can be satisfied with a few moments of greatness, and his usual comment after such moments of psychic intoxication that fulfill all anxious expectation is: "the cork's out of the bottle"! The fact is that the essences of the psyche penetrate through the senses. José Bergamin, poet and *aficionado* and writer of an important book about the bulls, felt *the unheard music of bullfighting*.[13]

There was *temple,* too, in the *veronicas* performed by José Luis Vázquez. Six-and-a-half *veronicas* with *temple* that made possible the appearance of the Duende and touched the Duende of the spectators as well as that of the old *aficionado* who felt rejuvenated.

The appearance of the Duende as Lorca presents it, or as I have tried to exemplify it with these and subsequent images, is the way it emerges in explosive, expansive, open ways in extreme cases. But I think that we should not overlook other ways for the Duende to make its appearance, because they happen in the same context and correspond to more intimate emotions, the private affairs of the person who feels them. It happens when, both in bullfighting images and in the image made music in flamenco, we have feelings that affect our inner being, as if something were stirring inside us so that our eyes fill with tears, although we might manage to retain our composure. As the Andalusians say, what happens is "deep down inside" and accompanying it, we feel our psyche stirring and our soul forging itself. *Flamenco* offers us more intimate possibilities than revelry does. One occasionally sees two friends sitting at a table with a bottle of wine, singing to each other as if in whispers. And this gives us a very ancient, very Mediterranean image of the beauty of an Eros: a dialogue between two souls through the vehicle of *flamenco*. There are images in *flamenco* poetry that can easily be associated with dreams. The image occurs as if in

13. José Bergamin, *La Música Callada del Toreo* (Madrid: Turner, Tercera Edición, 1985).

a dream, as if it came from that unknown region whence dreams emerge and reach us, where dream and poetic image become one. There is another appearance of the Duende that should not be excluded. It comes when we are thrown off balance, disconcerted, which is what Andalusians describe as feeling *pasmo*. At such times, we feel as if Dionysus were offering his hand to Hermes. It is a gust of air, an irrepressible instant, rather like a ghost that suddenly appears and then vanishes again just as abruptly. In the same way, the mind is invaded by certain intangible images of death, of an evanescent subtlety that leave us dumbfounded. It is those inner ghosts that are ineffable.

I write these lines in an attempt to bring Lorca's legacy alive by way of annotations, reflections and amplifications, of what the Duende moves and in so doing to propitiate an access to acceptance of his contribution and if possible to expand it. I would like to take from Lorca, or, to put it another way, to rob him hermetically of everything I can, using what is thieved to enrich us. In two meaning-crammed lines, Lorca defines the very core of the art of bullfighting, which, in tauromachy, would require an entire treatise: "The bull has its orbit; the bullfighter has his, and between the two orbits is a danger point where the vertex of the terrible game is."[14] These lines move us to deeper and consequently very mature reflections. In synthesis, they transmit to us the most intimate knowledge of bullfighting, that of the territories and distances in the ring, the only thing which avoids the ugly scenes of the matador being trampled underfoot and the painful mishaps, and makes *temple* and the Duende possible: something we can steal from Lorca and tauromachy, and which is of value in life itself, not to mention its value in psychotherapy, where missionary inroads into the territories of the patient stifle and do not allow the psychic side to breathe, trampling on it and preventing the psyche from being lived psychically.

On the other hand, what Lorca says about the appearance of the Duende in *flamenco* cannot be improved upon. There *is,*

14. Federico García Lorca, *op. cit.,* p. 119.

however, one image that greatly impressed me and lingers on in my mind, though I read it a long time ago in a treatise on flamenco. A group of flamenco singers (among them, the celebrated Don Antonio Chacón) was having a night out in Madrid, when it suddenly occurred to one of them to summon Manuel Torre from Andalusia. Presumably, Torre arrived in Madrid some time the next day. He walked into the party and sat down in a corner to listen to the other revellers singing. One of them sang a couplet, upon which Manuel Torre stood up and sang a single line of the same couplet, and at once, the madness of the Duende took possession of everyone present. This image of Torre is like the one described by Lorca when the prize for a dancing competition at Jerez de la Frontera was awarded to an old lady of eighty: "for simply raising her arms, throwing back her head and stamping her foot on the boards." That is an image sending us in other directions, because it shows that the psyche of the Dionysian body is present in old age and helps us towards a better, deeper understanding of the meaning of the dance of the two old men, Tiresias and Cadmus, in the *Bacchae* of Euripides. This image obviously demonstrates that the Dionysian psychic body continues into old age. Moreover, and we shall confirm this further on, the deepest Dionysian complexities are disclosed only in old age. It has always impressed me that Euripides wrote the *Bacchae,* the most impressive testimony to things Dionysian, when he was almost eighty and living in Macedonia in exile from his beloved Athens.

There is, however, one thing which I might mention here and that is ritual, the appropriate ritual to the Duende which exists in *flamenco*. Revelry is propitiated by a spontaneous happening. The soul needs Duende as nourishment, but the soul is nourished by what happens spontaneously: that is how revelry begins. People eat and drink and sing and sing again; they move from one place to another, some drop out, others join in. It all adds up to a propitiatory Dionysian ritual, in the hope that the invocation, the wine, the purpose of the song, will bring about that moment of Duende that revives us and gives meaning to the happening: "The arrival of the Duende always presupposes a radical change in all the forms on old levels, it conveys sensations of wholly unprecedented freshness, with the quality of a recently created rose, of a miracle, producing an almost religious fervor."[15] In both *flamenco* and bullfighting, this revival and death are not separate. When we speak of a rebirth in terms of revival in our conception of the Duende, experience which is lived is linked with the images that specifically pertain to the imagery of death. Thus, rebirth is inconceivable without the imagery that associates us with death.

Experiencing danger in bullfighting or a *cante jondo* that comes to us from "the dark and terrifying depths" makes us sense that the image we perceive originates in the archetypal realm, from where life acquires meaning and is revived with death. Flamenco dancing, in the ultimate meaning, alludes to death; the image that male or female dancers show us when the Duende appears speaks of a tearing apart, a Dionysian dismemberment, the essence of Dionysian madness. And here we are in the precincts of a madness of death imagery that teaches us to die. That is how we feel those moans, laments and that rending of garments mentioned by Lorca.

The relationships between Dionysian madness and death await exploration, but let us leave this for now as a mere reference and, with Lorca's text, feel the weight of the image, of an image in opposition to the thousand lectures. No one has described this better and more boldly than the Venezuelan writer on bullfighting, Carlos Villalba. In July 1976, in the Caracas daily *El Nacional,* he wrote a splendid article about the death of Heidegger which is extremely apposite to our theme. Villalba tells us that a bull's two horns say more about death than all the philosophers' works on Being and Death. He tells us that philosophers do not know what they are *dealing with* when they talk about death, that bullfighters, the image-makers of death, are the true masters to impart instruction on the initiation into death: for a single image will tell us more about death than a host of philosophical theories. Villalba writes that the *corrida*

15. *Ibid.,* p. 113.

also contains a body of "teaching about death," and it seems that the Duende haunts his words.

As to the Duende and death, allow me to introduce the reader to someone who is a most relevant figure in Lorca's work: *El llanto por la muerte de Ignacia Sánchez Mejías*[16, 17] is one of the century's classic poems, and the reading public gets to know Ignacio Sánchez Mejías through Lorca's great poem about a subject which has long been a great source of inspiration for poets – bulls and bullfighting. In order to bring out some elements of the personality of Sánchez Mejías, whose death inspired the poem, I think it is worthwhile to approach the place where the Duende and death brush against each other: a lament turned poem, a poem with Duende, and in this case with two protagonists, the bullfighter who dies, and the poet. In his *History of Bullfighting,* Nestor Luján says: "When we come to the biography of Ignacio Sánchez Mejías, we must employ a different tone from that used for any other bullfighter who ever existed. For Ignacio Sánchez Mejías was without equal as a bullfighter and as a man."[18] Thus it is by no means easy to trace in broad outlines a personality so complicated "as a bullfighter and as a man," to attempt to bring the reader close to Lorca's innermost being and and intuition of the Duende.

Ignacio Sánchez Mejías was born into a well-to-do family. He was the son of a doctor, something quite unusual among bullfighters, who nearly always come from the lower classes, "the social outcasts." Lorca calls Ignacio "the well-born." Although he began to fight bulls as a young child in the little ring of the farm attached to his house with none other than Joselito, the greatest bullfighter of all time, who later became his friend and brother-in-law (Ignacio married Lola, Joselito's younger sister), it can be said that he was not born a bullfighter

16. *Ibid.,* p. 537.
17. Brian Vickers, in his book, *Towards Greek Tragedy* (p. 88) says: "It is remarkable how much of Greek Tragedy – and how much of the greatest poetry – is in essence a lament for the dead."
18. Néstor Luján, *Histria del Toreo* (Barcelona: Destino), p. 294.

in the usual sense of the word. He had to make himself one, he had to learn the hard way, and every appearance in the ring was a struggle with himself and the crowd, which drove him to attempt incredible feats. "[He was] a rather clumsy bullfighter, with a Dionysian presence and boundless recklessness. He was a matador who was dominant in the ring and led an adventurous and restless life. High-spirited and endowed with great vitality, he dedicated himself to the bulls because in the period when he was born in Seville, bullfighting was the only glamorous and romantic avenue open to a hero. In another age, he might have been a *conquistador,* a smuggler or a warrior.... He lived a legendary life among dancers, bullfighters and poets, and in addition he was one of the most fervent and effective sources of inspiration of the magnificent generation of poets before the Civil War."[19] This alone gives us a glimpse of a personality who made his presence felt, who stimulated and was able to move the soul of poets. A great patron of *flamenco,* he protected the old dancers and brought some of them back into fashion. As a result, La Malena, La Macarrona (immortalized by Picasso) and the old, crippled Fernanda returned to the boards. His hacienda was a refuge for the purest *flamenco* where Manuel Torre, the last great singer, in whom flamenco turned into mythology, could be heard. It is said that Ignacio once telephoned Lorca at dawn so that he could hear the brilliant heel-clicking of "la Argentinita." He was also a writer and his play, *Without Reason,* was performed in Madrid in 1928. Cossío said of it: "The bullfighter does not tackle a minor middle-class theme that is more or less tangential to the bullfighting milieu. Instead, he deliberately confronts a problem of madness or reason and unfolds the complications of the plot with considerable elegance."[20] Here Cossío is telling us that Ignacio was at ease with the irrational. He also wrote a comedy, *Zayas,* which was staged in Santander in the same year. As a bullfighter, he shared the bill with "the best of his time, that is to say, the best of all

19. Néstor Luján, *ibid.*
20. José María de Cossío, *op. cit.,* p. 875.

times." As a *banderillero*, he was exceptional, brilliant. In this *suerte* his personality and courage were stretched to the limit: he complicated it, provoking difficulty, risking himself and creating emotion. Here his Duende appeared, bringing us closer to the imagery of death. Ignacio Sánchez Mejías, said those who knew him and saw him fight, "did not know the meaning of danger," as if the equation, "danger=death" did not exist for him. Hemingway, who also knew him, says that a year before Ignacio died, the *flamenco* Gypsies of the "Villarosa" in Madrid could smell the death he carried with him. When his son wanted to become a bullfighter, he flew into a rage and said: "I am the only one who will enter this house killed by the horns of a bull." This not only enables me to trace the outline of a personality, but also to reflect on the Dionysian from its most exalted and most vital extremes.

García Lorca was Dionysian too. He belonged to a world of poets, bullfighters and flamenco artists. Lorca was a poet, a musician and a man of the theater. His genius was expressed through the Dionysian. He repeatedly sang to death and wrote about the Duende. His actual death is a theme of our time. By this, I mean that it is prime material for study and reflection; to me, Lorca's death is a scene on the stage of the World Theater, the place which makes archetypal reflection possible.

José Antonio Rial, in his play *The Death of García Lorca*,[21] a stage version of Irish writer Ian Gibson's book, *The Assassination of García Lorca*,[22] (the definitive book about Lorca's death by firing squad), suggests an imaginative finale that coincides with what I feel, especially when he makes us see the shooting of Lorca as a bullfight worthy of an ear and a tail, as if death in the ring and death, no matter how, in the Spanish Civil War, were one and the same thing. The praises of the bull's death, turned into a Dionysian, primordial ritual, receive here

21. José Antonio Rial, *La muerte de García Lorca,* (Caracas: Monte Avila C.A., 1975).
22. Ian Gibson, *The Assassination of Federico García Lorca* (Penguin Books, 1983).

their greatest expression. Moreover, these words are put into the mouth of the *banderillero* Galadí (Lorca died alongside two *banderilleros*, Galadí and Arcollas, and a lame schoolmaster, Dióscuro Galindo González; his grave digger was a Gypsy). That is how I feel and this is where my feeling takes me: to see the Spanish Civil War as a great mythological *corrida*. I do not feel any irreverence in Rial nor extravagance in my attitude. Moreover, in this century's painting, the greatest masterpiece is Picasso's *Guernica*, where the tragedy of the Spanish Civil War, and Picasso's personal emotions are fused with elements of the *corrida*, expressed in the drama enacted by the horse and the bull. Besides: "No one can fully understand the history of Spain from 1650 to the present day unless they have rigorously constructed the history of bullfighting in the strictest sense of the word; not the bullfighting *fiesta* which has existed in one form or another for three millennia, but what we call by that name today."[23] These are the words of a man, Ortega y Gasset, who used to say when he went to the bullfight: "I'm going to see how Spain is getting on." I prefer this madness to the other madness with which the Spanish Civil War has been viewed, since we do not need to step outside the inner world of psyche and divide ourselves into factions in order to refer to what is happening in the world, nor do we need to take sides in order to express ourselves. The curse of taking sides is in choosing and compromising with an easily accessible madness (an accursed, titanic madness); what is difficult is the other madness...

Now let us remember the first lines of the essay on the Duende, of burning importance to me, because they make me feel Lorca's struggle to rid his soul of the titanic sterility of those "thousand lectures" and of everything comprised by what we call *ideology,* and let us recognize that this too is Dionysian.[24]

23. Carlos Orellana, ed. (Madrid: Orel, 1969).
24. It is quite impossible for me to conceive of Dionysus as preaching ideology. His epiphany, when it occurs collectively, takes place among a group of maenads, in drunken revelry, before the Battle of Salamis or during Spain's National Fiesta, in a bullring, or in the soul of the ordinary man.

To me, to confine the death of Federico García Lorca within the bounds of the conflicting parties in the Spanish Civil War is utterly simplistic in this day and age. The consciousness of present-day man is sufficiently remote from the political romanticism of the Thirties. Reflection becomes possible at a distance of nearly half a century. Leaving the conflict within the environment of the conflicting factions seems to me at best like pointing out or localizing the madness in a world full of titanic repetitions, a madness that is, as I have said, an arena and stage propitious for killing other madnesses. Archetypally, Dionysus will always be the persecuted and dismembered deity, the most repressed of all the gods (Euripides says that he was even repressed in Thebes, the mythical birthplace of his mother), regardless of the political regime under which he lives; it is part of his essence.

It is in this connection that a topic of our time seems like an historical enactment of an eternal mythologem: the persecution and killing of Dionysus by the Titans echoed by the shooting of a great poet.[25] That is how García Lorca's death touches me as an element of consciousness. The historical elements provide me with a frame of reference, a field where the mythological drama is re-enacted. The mythological image of the persecution and dismemberment of Dionysus by the Titans makes for a *primordial image* that stands out for me. And if we were to confine such a fact solely to the sphere of the struggles of political factions, we would be most ingenious, since it would be like confining what are really very ancient conflicts and mythological battles to racial and social conflicts. As we are trying to show in these pages, these are the conflicts that make for the persecution and mortal dismemberment of Dionysus by the Titans. From the vantage point of this complex mythologem, and by trying to keep the focus on the images I am discussing, I attempt to approach intuitively the death of a human being in today's world. We live in a world whose history has stifled the

---

25. When referring to Lorca in his autobiography, *My Last Sigh*, Buñuel said: "He was the greatest of us all."

images which would serve as a means of access and nourish and sustain us in the "moment of truth," in that "supreme suerte" which is death. The images propitious for the process of dying are in retreat, devalued, utterly routed (but the Dionysian has always been fleeing, shamefully undervalued, defeated; such are its essential attributes). However, to have any connection with them, we must retire to a corner of our soul, which in the geography of our nature (soul in body and human nature) would be analogous to that corner of the outer world, i.e., Andalusia. There, if we are lucky enough to encounter the Duende, it will enable us to feel more intensely and enliven our soul as it approaches death, teaching it to die a Dionysian death.

Much theorizing and writing about death is going on in the West. So much so that a recent book, almost a best-seller, deals with the history of that subject.[26] When the historians recount the rich imagery of death in the Middle Ages we are amazed; yet in so doing, they are also pointing out the element of dying that has been discarded. Death, as it appeared to western man in the Catholic world, was a passage to a beyond, and a confession, a reassuring rite (the presence of a religious element or guarantee of death at peace with one's conscience), was like a safe passage to the promised happiness of a Christian heaven. All added to that, in the Catholic world, the imagery of passion and death, with the central image of the agony, is also fading, not to mention the Protestant world, where it is conspicuous by its absence. Today death is in the hands of medical technology and we know that technological titanism does not recognize death. The memory of death in the soul is absent. Thus, it seems as if the image of the agony cannot even be conceived of now and is therefore no longer respected. In religious Christianity, there was no death as such; only passage to another world, and in Christian technology, there is no longer even that. Here, death has lost its meaning altogether, including respect for the agony that makes possible the appearance of the Duende.

26. Philippe Aries, *La Muerte en Occidente* (Barcelona: Edit. Argos Vergara, 1982).

For this reason all the things that Lorca says in his *Theory and Play of the Duende* are so vitally important for present-day man, in as much as they are intuitions of the soul, of the greatest interest to him and, of course, to psychotherapy. Instead of dwelling on naïve and uncultured speculations about childhood and the initial trauma (after all, we are born as we are born, we grow up as best we can within the historical complexes that affect us and we function in life with more than one foot in the mystery of our own nature), death and its imagery are valued more highly than the puerilities of birth and childhood. It is a psychotherapeutic vision that makes us feel the efforts of the pioneers as very remote. We have death before our eyes and we feel, and by feeling we know, that our inner relationship with death tells us much more about our psychic conflicts and more still about the obscurity of our psychosomatic complaints than all the reductive dredging up of our childhood in which we may indulge.

If we adapt these reflections, which have much to do with current psychotherapy, to the equation of death=Duende which we have been discussing, we shall open our soul to valuation by feeling: the *spectrum* of catharsis. It shows great impoverishment of imagination that catharsis in psychotherapy is only accepted for what connects it with the confessional. Cathartic emotions appear in the Duende, as they do in Greek tragedy,[27] before the perfection of *certain* forms. Here I confine *forms* to the Dionysian. Ivan Linforth, in his excellent book, *The Arts of Orpheus*,[28] establishes that Dionysus is always the body. In whatever we call psychotherapy, the emotional catharsis is exhibited in the body and has an essential value, because we already know that what we call psychic body is inhabited by the gods most repressed by history. Hence, what comes from there

27. There is no doubt that bullfighting and Greek tragedy are essentially related in their forms. *Fear* and *pity* are emotions fundamental to both of them (Aristotle).
28. Ivan Linforth, *The Arts of Orpheus* (New York: Arno Press, N.Y. Times Comp., 1973).

is of capital importance; something which, in terms of the psychology of the opposites, would compensate for the historical repression of the psychic body, which makes for psychosomatic balance, thus facilitating an equilibrium between health and illness.

What matters for present-day man's soul is whether in his death there are a *few drops of the Dionysian essences* to bring a touch of joy to his dying. And this, mythologically and archetypally speaking, is in irreconcilable opposition to the infernal titanic Promethean machine and its appearance in our times in the guise of technological scientism. Mythologically and poetically speaking, Dionysus and the Titans are two aspects of human nature which exist in irreconcilable opposition and their imagery is that of a Dionysus in constant flight, trying to flee, to hide and defend himself from titanic aggression and excess. Titanic interference in the process of dying, technological dying with medical pretensions to "prolonging life," denies, or in any case, distorts a death which could give meaning to a whole life.

In the *Prometheus* of Aeschylus, the Titan Prometheus says clearly: "Yes, I caused men no longer to foresee their death." That shows us the titanic contempt for death. Of course, we are aware of this, because it is a topical theme in the newspapers and in our everyday conversations. And if we try to understand the Titan's interference with, or transgression in, something which does not concern him, the most difficult thing to understand (and the ultimate camouflage of horror) is when we start listening to talk about death (in some circles it is fashionable to talk and give lectures about it) with the same boredom as that of Lorca's thousand lectures. Thus, we hear of things that sound like prescriptions for 'how to die' or claiming to teach us how to 'manage' death, as if the aim were to deprive the whole affair of any significance. Alternatively, we are told that we must not be afraid of death. Dionysus is equated with Hades, Heraclitus says, and Dionysus is the only god who is afraid and does not hide the fact. Indeed, he shows his fear, but fear as a tragic emotion that connects and vivifies us, not as a defect or cowardice.

It is possible that each archetype has its own conception of and approach to death. I am trying to distinguish between the different religious conceptions of dying, each of which corresponds to the forms of the god ruling it. This implies that we are delimiting the archetypal configurations around death, which would be to disregard the unique conception, feelings and experience of each human being in relation to death.

Let us return to the Duende and Lorca's equation, which states that whoever has Duende is also the bearer of death; because who will deny the fact that the moments propitious to the appearance of the Duende occur during the processes of death or at the critical moment of dying, the supreme *suerte*? And that this epiphany of the Duende is telling us what belongs to its moment? What tradition and the philosophers call "the meaning of life" is preserved in the deepest of Dionysian initiations, to be felt only at the moment of dying and in a state of Duende... "the Duende will not come unless it sees the possibility of death, unless it knows that it has to haunt his house, and unless it is sure that it has to shake the branches that we all carry and that are inconsolable now and forever."[29] This belongs to the realm of divine intervention: Dionysus making his epiphany at the time that belongs to him, and we are powerless because, faced with the divinity, mortals that we are, we must accept *his* intervention. And as a mortal, the only thing I venture to say, in bullfighting language, with a hint of Duende and out of the conflict and the fear in the face of that intervention, is that "I'll do my best."

---

29. Federico García Lorca, *op. cit.*, p. 117.

CONSCIOUSNESS OF FAILURE

Dedicated to Adolf Guggenbühl-Craig

In a world in which success-oriented propositions and formulas are the staple fodder, writing an essay entitled "Consciousness of Failure" puts the writer in diametrical opposition to the pressing demands of the collective consciousness. The theme I want to reflect on, however, is the product of a psychic movement that puts pressure on us from within, so that we become aware of what I call here the Consciousness of Failure. For the fact is that failure as a subject for discussion is excluded from the anxieties of our time. Failure and its attendant circumstances are severely repressed; it is as if it were the last thing we want to hear about.

Consciousness of failure has been haunting me for years. Undoubtedly the subject is connected with my practice as a psychotherapist, which has made it a little easier for me to realize that if people come to see and talk to me – in other words, to undertake psychotherapy – it is because something in their life has failed. The way in which they have been living no longer functions. The person sitting opposite me during psychotherapy is experiencing a failure that usually hides unsuspected complications, in spite of the superficial levels at which it sometimes appears. There is a big difference, however, between calling this failure by name and moving towards an awareness of it. What we euphemistically call crisis or something similar, secure in the reductive knowledge that a crisis can be easily resolved, can, in reality, be altering a whole life, whether we perceive it or not. On the other hand, failure or crisis does not always give life a new meaning or direction. For about fourteen or fifteen years, during my studies and in my discussions about cases with other psychotherapists, I have used such phrases as "Yes, so-and-so's psychotherapy is under way, but there is a long way to go yet; above all, he lacks a consciousness of failure." The fact that someone comes into psychotherapy having failed in life does not necessarily mean that he is really aware of that failure. It is even less likely that he is reconciled to it as the propitiatory vehicle propelling him towards what we are calling Consciousness of Failure. Often a patient expects, and even demands, that psychotherapy support and reinforce his fantasies of success. But sometimes (which is even worse) much of present-day psychotherapy is reduced to bolstering up the one-sided devotion to success in which the patient has lived, cleaning him reductively of everything that opposes success as a personal and collective goal.

Although I have been referring to these ideas for the last fifteen years at least, knowing full well that they have been on my mind for much longer, I have never before ventured to put them forward. It is as if the whole business actively 'refused' to be dealt with. Although I have used the term colloquially, it does not mean that it is entirely clear to me. Moreover, if the patient finds it difficult to accept or even pronounce the word, 'failure,' the same thing happens to the psychotherapist. If there is a consciousness, it is better that we call it a 'certain' consciousness, or an intuition, discarding any claim to a clear definition and accepting its inherent obscurity. Psychotherapists themselves may be the best people to understand what I am trying to say, because I find it ridiculous to conceive of a psychotherapist who identifies with his "successes" and has a "triumphalist" attitude; he must inevitably identify himself with the failures as well, unless he divides this mechanism of success and failure, like a man cutting an apple in half, and naively imagines that the successes are his and the failures the patient's. The model I propose appeared in my book, *Hermes and His Children*. It consists of the psychotherapist serving a process ruled by archetypes constellated in psychotherapy, archetypes through which human nature is expressed psychically in a process in which the time and *tempo* of the therapist-patient relationship fluctuates: two distinct alchemies which have unfathomable complexities, yet make the happening of psychotherapy possible.

The answer to the question of why failure so stubbornly refuses to be recognized has to be sought in the complex intricacies of human nature. This is the crucial point, and we psychologists cannot afford to miss it. We cannot lose sight of the fact that in dealing with so-called psychological material, we are dealing with human nature.

It is easy to see that historically the family, society and the collective demand are interested solely in success. It seems as if, in the confusion created by the necessity to survive, success has become the farthest extremity of the luminous pole that Western man experiences. It is a polarization that has left behind the opposite pole, where a large part of our nature still lies buried. We have failed to realize that we can only survive if we keep in touch with our nature and strive to make it the guiding principle in our survival. Consequently, if our aim is to achieve consciousness of failure, we should be more disposed to understand it as a consciousness trying to be reconciled with something that is obscure: the suffering in a part of our nature that has been rejected. Seen from the polarization of collective consciousness, everything comprised by the word *failure* is repressed and discarded; the collective calls only for success. We demand success and the demand is so imperious that we must succeed at all costs, leaping whatever barriers may stand in our way. The only slogan is success, and often success is transformed into duty. Once the demand is for success at all costs, success is ripe for conversion into automatism. It turns into a slogan and becomes an autonomous complex. Thus success is not necessarily bound up with the possible delimitations of an individual nor with any earthly reality. We are required to succeed in everything we set out to do. When the need to succeed is a forgone conclusion, leading to repetition, we fall victims to the misguided fancy that we deserve success.

In this extreme position, we lose contact with any possibility of reflection, and anything that we understand by success becomes irreflective, thus distancing us from the basic patterns of earthly reality. What I call 'earthly reality' comes from a term coined by Janet early in the century – *la fonction du réel*. It was incorporated by Jung into his psychiatric studies when he observed the lack of this function in psychotic and schizophrenic patients. In this essay, I wish to use it in a similar way to Jung, so that it may serve as a backdrop against which we can see the element of madness inherent in this *lack of earthly reality*. In most cases, it is a madness not to be found in mental hospitals, but which reveals itself in the vision offered to us by the triumphalist autonomy of the world we live in. Nevertheless, it is easy to accept that this lack of reality is a part of the so-called normal personality, but can only be diagnosed as such when it erupts on a large scale, thus altering the personality. It is in this way that we can observe and register it. How this psychic reality exists in so-called 'normality,' what affect it has psychically and psychosomatically and whether it plays a part in the equilibrium of that 'normality's' health and existence depends upon the criteria of the observer.

The possibility of failure does not enter into what we call the collective consciousness and its demands. When there is a collapse that we could see as a failure from which we could learn and reflect, we rapidly rebound from it by clutching at another vain fantasy, advancing irrevocably to meet another failure. For what might save us from new failures is consciousness of the previous failure; failure providing reflection. But no, the demand for success is so enslaving that it does not leave us the time or the *tempo* that makes reflection possible. The demand for success, transformed into an autonomous complex, impels us to repetition. One of the great contributions to the psychology of this century is the theory of the complexes, which says that a complex (a slice of history) which is not reflected upon and made conscious, repeats itself in a potentialized and hypertrophied form.

During infancy and adolescence, the psychic dynamic is one

of competitive, success-oriented emulation: success in studies, sports, among one's friends, in one's life. Competition, rivalry, envy and emulation have their rightful biological age in adolescence and form a field where success and success-oriented fantasies reign. Such adolescent fantasies harbor a certain futurism that is appropriate to this stage. An example might be of an older adolescent dreaming of getting his degree, marrying, taking a post-graduate degree, having a family and making a success of life. These are the fantasies and formative projects befitting the psychology of that age, and they are valid, although many of them have to be modified before the age of thirty: the marriage fails, success in one's profession is not as easy as was imagined, and there are unmistakable signs of depression and even of destruction, with an imagery quite the opposite of the success-seeker's.

So the fantasies and projects that are an important combination in the average adolescent (for the readers' information I am omitting the large element of destructiveness usually present in adolescence) sometimes continue into adulthood. They are perpetuated, and we see grown men in their late thirties or early forties, and even over fifty, who are living the same fantasy that may well have been valid in their adolescence. In wanting to retain those same impulses and the same speed they once had, they show clearly that there have been shortcomings, paralysis in the process of psychic initiation into adulthood.

The processes I refer to were seen from the evolutionist point of view by William Sheldon, who wrote about the subject in the years before the Second World War, when he was discussing these ideas with C.G. Jung in Zurich. With reference to William James, Sheldon writes: "He found mental growth so rare in the later decades of life that a matured intellect seemed to stand out as a curiosity . . . ." Thirty years later, Sheldon wrote:

Today the situation is apparently worse. The days of youth sometimes teem with morning dreams, ennobling plans; but the human mind at forty is commonly atrophied, deadened, wasteful of its hours – not infrequently poisoned, as with alcohol or drugs. Yet there are a few who progress toward full mental growth. At twenty these do not particularly stand out, except that they often seem socially immature for their age. But at thirty-five or forty it can be gathered from a half a dozen sentences that here are minds still alive. The philosophy is tentative and sensitive, interests are expanding, there is an eagerness for new knowledge.

People who show these qualities in mid-life are inclined to continue their mental growth for the rest of the way, often gathering headway and competence even in the final decade. For such, a year in the seventies or eighties may be worth, in both affective and cognitive fulfillment, far more than a year of youth. These few live more for the second than for the first half of life. They seem happier and intrinsically stronger in old age than in youth. Their lives suggest an uneasy intuition that where youth is a disproportionately happy period, life may be a great failure.

The above shows that our theme belongs to the spirit of the age in which there is more than one consciousness which knows how to appreciate failure as the source of new consciousness. Thus, Education, the Academy and the University are regions reigned over by Apollo, the god who personifies the unilateral nature of the brilliance and success-orientation which dominates life. Nevertheless, I know a university professor running a seminar on Planning who, before accepting a new student, makes it a necessary condition for his studies that the candidate proves he has failed in something and understands that having failed and accepted the failure denotes an aptitude. He explained that as Planning *per se* is such an abstract, accelerated affair, with a highly Apollonic vision, a concomitant global vision, and consequently a tendency towards psychic inflation, a failure was the least he could ask of potential students as an indispensable, compensatory credential. And failure in the example I have just given can easily be regarded as an anchor linking the student somehow with earthly reality.

Thus, in psychological and psychotherapeutic studies (I refer specifically to commentaries on the experience of the Jung Institute in Zurich), those who turn out to be the worst psychotherapists, with the most boring theories and writings, whose personal contributions to psychological studies have been of little value, are precisely those students whose matriculation at the Institute was based on the selection of *curricula summa cum laude,* that is to say, students who began to study psychology from the brilliant, success-oriented angle, without amending their one-sidedness in the course of their own studies and psychotherapy. This is a serious defect in a psychology which is primarily based on reading the image it is confronted with and the unconscious content which accompanies that image. It is a psychology which needs to learn from the darker side, the opposite and repressed side, and to have a consciousness ready to recognize and value it. This quality may be more important than ever today, since the studies of Jungian psychology have moved away from the spiritual, mercurial aspect, which was the characteristic of the Zurich maestro, to the chthonic, terrene and subterranean. By this we mean hermetic movements whose dominant feature is gravitational: a Hermes who brings us closer to the exploratory intuition of the unconscious as human body and nature.

There are three strong elements in human nature: the *Puer Aeternus,* hysteria and the psychopathic component, with acceleration as the dominant feature of their expression, a feature which is closely bound up with irreflection. When the three elements dominate the personality, it tends to identify itself with them, losing the ability to keep them at a distance which would propitiate the stirring of reflection. Here we see reflection as one of the five instincts which, according to Jung, inhabit the human being: hunger, sexuality, doing things, reflection and creativity. We must distinguish the instinct of reflection from what is called 'spiritual reflection,' which consists in reflecting within the bounds of a religious tradition and the norms of the life of what we call 'civilized man.' The instinctive reflection to which I refer is central to Jungian psychotherapy. In our own day, Alfred Ziegler wrote: "Reflection is actually hermeneutic, the art of phenomenological interpretation –

as easy as it is difficult. It seems to be the simplest thing in the world and at the same time the most complex."[1] But a minimum of time is required for the reflection to take place and to produce the *tempo,* the slow pace at which reflection happens, and that is only possible within the complexities of the nature of each individual.

The three elements which we are going to discuss are seen as an integral part of human nature; they provoke *hubris* (transgression) and, as we have said, make reflection difficult. Two of them – the *Puer Aeternus* and hysteria – are archetypal, which means they belong to archetypal configurations of our nature. The third, the psychopathic component of personality, though not archetypal, and having no forms to contain it, is also part of human nature. These three components can be studied and experienced in different ways. In many cases, the three are confused, and we sometimes observe people who exhibit a veritable conglomeration of these elements. In other cases, one of the three stands out from the rest; yet other cases which, if we are able to observe them for a sufficient length of time, begin in youth with the dominant *Puer Aeternus,* reinforced to excess by hysterical histrionics and later, in adult years, lapse into the repetitive round of the psychopathic.

The *Puer Aeternus,* the eternal adolescent, rules the life of the child and the adolescent archetypally. The *Puer,* with his brilliance and velocity, appears in archetypal studies in different ways. For our purposes, we shall consider him in opposition to the *Senex,* i.e., old age with its attendant limitations, slowness, chronic illness and existing on the threshold of death. Also in this discussion, we shall exclude his relationship with the mother. It must always be remembered, however, that no matter how obvious and complicated, conflictive and chaotic it may be, the *Puer's* relationship with the mother is archetypal and consequently incommensurable. Seen in this way, it is a relationship which contains the infinite possibilities conferred on it

---

1. *Archetypal Medicine*, trans. Gary V. Hartman (Spring Publications: Dallas), 1983, p. 45.

by this order, and which proclaims the absurdity of any kind of reduction. We know that mother and child are central figures in the realm of religion and the subject of studies of comparative religions. The image of the child which we contemplate on the altar of a Catholic Church in the arms of the youthful virgin mother is the Christian version of the *Puer Aeternus*. Sometimes the child holds a ball crowned with a cross in his hand as a symbolic attribute. This child in his essential relationship with his mother, as a vital feature of the religious world and also in our psyche and emotional body, is the transformed Christian version of those *Pueri* of the mythologies of antiquity, lovers of the Great Mother: Tammuz, Oumuzi and Marduk in Mesopotamia; Adonis in Phoenicia; Attis in Asia Minor; and Osiris in Egypt. In the classical Greek legacy, Kerényi and Jung worked on the *Puer,* taking it for granted that all the gods were *Pueri,* divine children. The divine child is central to Western culture, and if he is central both religiously and psychically, he is presumably also central to the pathology of Western man. Insighted in this way, we sense in the *Puer's* long, profound history, the complex backgrounds which we all carry within us.

For our purposes, we must confine ourselves to the opposites: *Puer - Senex* [youth and old age]. The *Puer* and *Senex* form a two-headed archetype in an essential polarity, which makes them one and the same – two sides of the same coin, unable to exist without each other. There is no *Puer* without *Senex,* no *Senex* without *Puer.* Hence, in Jungian studies of the archetypes, they are considered within this essential polarity. As far as we are concerned, they correspond to juvenile recklessness and speed, and to the slowness and limitations of old age. They mark the calendar life; that is to say, they make us feel, more or less accurately, our chronological age and our psychological age. They are constantly adjusting both the psychical and the physical speed of our life. Another manifestation is when they dominate the personality, which then falls into the narrow limitation of seeing all of life's other possibilities from only the *Puer/Senex* consciousness. The dominance of the *Puer/Senex* archetype totally blocks access to any other archetypal form of life and, in psychotherapy, shows the repetitive, pitiful image referred to by Sheldon of living a life solely within the confines of the *Puer/Senex* model and rhetoric.

The *Puer* makes us feel that there is a mental speed in adolescence which, among other things, enables man to learn what he has to learn at that age and which is linked to the curiosity of trying to discover the world. It is studied as a speed of consciousness making possible the multiple connections which are the delight, enrichment, intoxication and fantasy of the adolescent. It produces the miracle, the ecstasy, out of which the *Puer's* mental flights lead him to fantasize that he holds 'the world in his hand,' while making him see old men as slow, decrepit and incapable. It is when he is extremely polarized that we feel the *Puer's* most immediate problem – the fact that he is prodigiously unconscious of the *Senex,* the other pole he has within himself – so much so that he generally projects it, mostly in an attempt to invalidate what does not belong to his time and *tempo,* what does not come within what he considers the novelty of his fantasy. We should never lose sight of the fact that, if these extreme velocities of the *Puer's* consciousness are an essential part of his nature, the more rapid his consciousness is, the slower the elements of the *Senex* inhabiting his unconscious will be. The *Puer's* central problem is that his mind acts so fast that he cannot feel the gravitational pull needed to connect to the archetypes with a different speed to his own. Neither does he feel, of course, the gravitation pull of the chthonic gods, which are in exclusive opposition to the flying *Puer.* Flight and freeing oneself are inherent to the *Puer's* nature. Marie-Louise von Franz has given us an image of the flying *Puer* in her interpretation of St. Exupéry's *Le Petit Prince,* a masterpiece dealing with this aspect of the archetype, showing us a conception of the *Puer's* flight transformed into art. The Little Prince, living high up in his world of asteroids, provides a dramatic and desolate image of someone who has lost hold of the earth, someone who has absolutely no connection with *earthly reality.*

This image, taken from literary art, can be conveyed into a psychological picture that highlights the superficiality of the psychology of the *Puer Aeternus*: the psychologist whose nature has impelled him all his life to remain possessed by the *Puer* archetype. Such a person conceives the studies of psychology and the practice of psychotherapy solely through the conflicts of the many theories he comes across, falling repeatedly into the most up-to-date and fashionable theory, forgetting that, as Jung said, psychotherapy is a praxis. If we are going to see this in terms of theory, then each patient needs his or her own theory. The *Puer* psychologist even discusses the psychology of the body, leading one to ask oneself, "How is it possible that a man whose consciousness is moving at that speed and who is so polarized up in the sky can talk or write about the body, a subject in such opposition to his flights and ideas?"

From the preceding pages, I think the reader will find it easy to imagine that today the *Puer Aeternus* is experiencing his golden age, with actualities that go far, far beyond his psychic flight, insuring him a promising future. We live in an age of space flights, and the *Puer's* future is one of Star Wars, wars which have little to do with terrestrial conflicts and which will be won or lost wholly within the *Puer's* field.

The psychology of the *Puer* develops at such a speed that it loses touch with the gravitational aspect of the earth and the low speeds that that enforces. In order for the *Puer's* high speeds to touch down on the earth, a process of descent must take place, a gradual gliding, until there is a reconciliation with earthly reality. That is what should happen 'normally,' but the descent often takes place brusquely. Something happens in the *Puer's* life which forces him to adopt lower speeds, more appropriate to the earth, and suddenly confront the earthly reality which his nature has desperately tried to avoid. This brusque readjustment is often accompanied by profound traumas or painful changes in his personality. But that is not always so, for sometimes the adolescent's psychology is perpetuated beyond the limits fixed by the cycles of nature, with the support of societies in which juvenile ideals are dangerously dominant, and all the fantasy and imagery is projected from the sphere of the adolescent. Nowadays, for example, we have societies in which eating habits, clothes, personal aesthetics, etc., indeed life as a whole, is controlled by adolescent imagery and fantasy. When the individual, as well as societies in which the adolescent predominates as the collective ideal, totally disregard the opposite earthly pole, they seek to compensate for it, and generally do so destructively.

Nevertheless, the eternal adolescent lives in all of us and has a function to fulfill in our psychic life. It also has its sphere of creativity, which has been studied and which has manifested in some geniuses. We have only to think of Heisenberg at the age of nineteen, who was sunbathing on the roof of his house in Berlin in the days of the Weimar Republic, when the theory of indetermination came to him out of the blue, amid sporadic bursts of anti-riot gunfire. Rimbaud, who wrote his poetic works at the age of nineteen or twenty, is another example. The fact is that the psychic speed of the *Puer* can appear in both abstract science and poetry, singling out a creative personality from a very early age, but not all the activities of human beings are suitable for the spectacular appearance of the *Puer*.

Thus, if by the study of the psyche we understand not only the study of existing theories, but also its relation to the continuous psychic formation of the person engaged in the study, the contribution of adolescent brilliance is minimal; it is absolutely scandalous to say that a person at the age of nineteen or thirty is a genius of the psyche, inasmuch as the study of the psyche requires, among other things, the psychic self-experience and reflection of the person studying it. This is fundamental and is only possible in the course of a long life. Moreover, studies of psychology offer the material *in vivo* of those who begin to study it when very young without the experience of life behind them. They attack established psychology and continue studying with pretensions to producing new theories with followers and schools, trying to apply titanic models of newfangled revolutionary panaceas to the subject. But some of us have lived long enough to see how so many of them have remained bogged down in these juvenile impulses, how their personal psyches never advanced, how their studies never progressed beyond the intuition with which the *Puer* in them conceived those studies. Now, in their riper years, they offer only the lamentable repetition of the ideas they conceived as young men.

I have tried to give the reader a brief survey, a summary adapted to the purpose of this paper, of an archetypal condition which is incommensurable and central to the history of religion and culture, and therefore inescapable in each one of us. We have all been children and adolescents, and although I have pointed out the elements of unreality and destruction in the *Puer*, this does not mean that I undervalue or despise this psychic element within us. Just as I have indicated the fatal consequences of its appearance as a dominant psychic element of the personality outside its rightful time, I should also mention that nature allots it a very important specific function in our mature years and old age, provided that the latter are lived in the reality of the age corresponding to them. Because he is an archetype, the *Puer* will accompany us to the end of our days.

Earlier I mentioned Sheldon and his evolutionist view of the stages of life; now I shall give a condensed version of the Jungian view. Jung was very much aware of the *Puer's* importance, and the School of Zurich has done intensive work on the subject. It was Jung himself who did the first work on the study of the *Puer,* and throughout his *œuvre* there are numerous references to the imagery of the *Puer Aeternus.* He saw that in cases where a more complete adulthood and old age were observed, the *Puer's* role and function were in harmony with the ages which were being lived through. But it is to Marie-Louise von Franz that we are indebted for the fundamental studies of the *Puer,* and much of what I want to say here is based upon her contributions (though I should add that I place psychopathy where she places the negative, destructive side of the archetype of the *Puer*). Viewed in isolation, the psychopath lacks the mental flights of the *Puer* and his imagery. To me, the relationship is one of mimesis. The psychopath mimics the inflated ideas of the *Puer,* both personally and collectively, and history is a living example of the latter.

We have already mentioned that, in adolescence and youth,

the *Puer* appears with a very rapid consciousness and at the same time, a very slow unconscious, which makes it impossible for him to shape what comes to his consciousness into the reality of an earthly form (here the words *conscious* and *unconscious* should be taken didactically, the first, meaning what comes from within the framework of our mental representations and the second, what is repressed, whether in the personal or collective field, or what is waiting to be experienced). But throughout life until the arrival of what could be considered a productive adulthood and old age, we observe a slow rotatory movement of these opposites. And where there was formerly speed, a slower consciousness begins to manifest itself, until it acquires a slowness adapted to the *tempo* of the psychic event which comes from within *and* of the event it faces in the external world. Consciousness slows down because the *Senex* is gradually occupying it, and while this is happening the velocities of the *Puer's* consciousness go on rotating until they take on an important role in the unconscious. So we can imagine how, throughout life, the images of *Puer* and *Senex* are inverted (to the rhythm of an hourglass) and supply another vital reality in adulthood and old age – that of a very slow consciousness, but a rapid active unconscious that has the necessary speed to connect with the memory stored there. The process of initiation into the second half of life – what Jung calls *metanoia* – is of capital importance for our studies, for we must never forget that the changes halfway through life are what give perspective, dimension and depth to the Jungian conception of life and, of course, to psychotherapy. It is that which preserves the analytic vision from causal fixations.

The eternal adolescent functions in the moment that belongs to him, enriching life, or tries to perpetuate himself beyond his archetypal age, holding back a personality by excess of identification with those elements. I now wish to mention the other archetypal psychic component that distorts the personality while indicating psychic acceleration. A characteristic of this component is that it does not encourage insights into a deeper relation with the complexes which could produce a more mature consciousness. Instead, it blocks the way to consciousness of failure.

The psychological studies of our century, a century which feels the need for psychic exploration, began with the studies of hysteria. I am not going to discuss Charcot, who attracted the best brains of the *fin de siècle* to his Paris studio, because they are of no interest to the subject presently being treated. The historical handbook is well-known and is not of great importance here. What I propose to do is to choose from among the countless conceptions of hysteria one which occurred to Jung around 1908 in the form of an image. Jung says that hysteria is like a platform from which all happenings rebound, preventing them from touching the complexes, from activating or animating them, from stirring them up and making possible psychic reflections, thus transforming them into experience. The first impression this image makes on us is one of superficiality, because everything that happens remains in the superficiality pertaining to hysteria and cannot penetrate beneath the surface to the fragments of personal history or the history of man on earth. But in this image, especially if the reader heightens his imagination a little, there is a sense of speed, the speed which the person whose life is dominated by hysteria must develop. He must be constantly bouncing against the surface of that hysterical platform, against that superficiality, without forming any relationship with psychic contents other than hysteria from which he could draw nourishment.

Since Jung wrote this, studies of hysteria have multiplied, and today we can say that the infinite web formed by these studies has not taken into account the hysterical point of view of the person studying hysteria. That is to say, none of the studies has taken into account personal hysterical projections onto what was being studied.

Today, however, hysteria is seen and studied as an archetypal component, and consequently belongs to all of us, men and women. So we can dispense with the misogyny that has dominated so many of these studies and caused hysteria to be seen as an affliction solely associated with women. We are indebted to

Niel Micklem's studies[2] when we say that hysteria is archetypal, and therefore we must admit that we are all hysterical to
some degree. I do not intend to enter into the complexities
which Micklem took as the starting point for his studies, as this
would go beyond the scope of the present discussion. My concern in this study is merely to show hysteria as blocking access
to consciousness of failure, although I do want to discuss the
most obvious and objective archetypal element of hysteria,
namely *suffocation*. This element was diagnosed in the 16th
century by an Englishman, Dr. Edward Jordan, in his book, *A
Brief Discourse of a Disease Called Suffocation of the Mother*.
His description of hysteria as the suffocation of the daughter by
the mother was based on an actual case, that of a fourteen-year-
old girl who had been bewitched by an old crone. It was, however, his work that put Micklem on the trail of the archetypal
study of hysteria. By reading the image of the mythologem of
mother and daughter, Demeter-Persephone, analogically, Micklem's work makes for a better approach to a psychic component, which expresses itself in all of us, in very different ways.
It appears in our everyday life in countless guises and may also
dominate a specific pathology.

We know that the study of hysteria made its appearance in
the earliest Western civilizations, Egypt and Greece, and has
existed throughout the two millennia of our own civilization.
Moreover, as we have said, it was the psychic condition which,
because it was immediately apparent, inaugurated modern studies of depth psychology. But in spite of being recognized for
centuries and so immediately perceptible in life, I am not claiming that it is always easy to recognize and even less that it is
easy to treat. Inasmuch as it is archetypal, hysteria is part of
human nature and incommensurable. It may and does appear in

---

2. For the sake of clarity, the aspects of hysteria I am going to reflect on
   here come from insights based on Niel Micklem's earlier work: "On
   Hysteria: The Hysterical Syndrome" (Spring, 1974). For the scope
   and purposes of the present study, this article is more than sufficient.
   For a more ample and differentiated view, I refer the reader to
   Micklem's forthcoming *Essays on the Nature of Hysteria*.

our everyday life in disguises and unusual forms that confuse even the person who is most aware of what is involved or who has the ability to detect its appearance and reflect upon it.

According to the great 16th century doctor, Thomas Sydenham: "Hysteria has more forms than Proteus and more colors than the chameleon," and is capable of simulating any thing or any illness. It is usually called the great simulator and is even considered capable of simulating the whole of life. It is difficult, but not impossible, to imagine that what we call life on earth is dominated by hysterical simulation and that even when we hear someone calling for an "authentic" life, we detect a note of hysterical simulation. But it is even more difficult for us to imagine a life without simulation, because it is an ingredient of human nature. Hysteria, be it an illness dominating the personality or a component we all possess, manifests itself capriciously, with unusual histrionics, but above all and significantly, it is tremendously irreflective and unconscious of itself. By irreflection, we mean here states of identification so unconscious that it is quite impossible for the hysteria (whether in a dominant, passive state or as a component appearing intermittently or veiled, altering life circumstantially) to be easily accessible to the patient's reflection or easily cured, for we must admit that this is not possible. The only thing capable of moving hysteria psychically and forcing it to emerge from its tiring repetitions is precisely what comes from the same mysterious and profound archetypal complexities to which hysteria belongs. We must limit ourselves to visualizing the archetypal image of mother and daughter: Demeter protecting her daughter Persephone from a presumptive ravisher, and in this act of protection, we can detect suffocation as the archetypal cause of hysteria. This belongs to the mythologem of the mother and daughter, which originated Kerényi's phrase, "The Greek Miracle," that miracle of having conceived ritually and initiatorily the archetype of the mother and daughter: the mysteries of Eleusis.

Thus, in spite of hysteria's irreflection and precisely because of it, its therapy must contain a large element of reflection. It is important to bear in mind that what I earlier called instinctive reflection has nothing to do with the clichés with pretensions to reflection. Within my own experience's limitations, reflection on hysteria must be focused on capturing the *image of suffocation* and on the patient's familiarizing himself with it until it becomes more or less psychic. And this is only as a psychotherapeutic base, because in reality the difficult thing about the psychotherapy of hysteria as a dominant is that it offers no possibility of creating the opposites where psychotherapy begins to make itself profound, to penetrate deeply into the patient's complexes and nature.

In the mythologem of mother and daughter, the rape of the daughter by the subterranean deity Pluto-Hades erupts as the opposite of the daughter's suffocation by the mother. It is a specific rape in the long catalogue of rapes in the Greek heritage, inasmuch as it is the imagination of death itself. It is Pluto, the personification of death, who rapes Persephone. Here we can equate rape with death, rape appearing in the psyche as the compensatory opposite to the superficial hysterical polarization. And we can certainly say that this moves life away from repetitive, destructive superficiality to depths where psychic life may begin to participate in corporeal life, creating the possibility of a consciousness which can distance itself from the mother, from what was formerly a suffocating hysterical identification. Rape is central to the psyche and the origins of culture.

The catalogue of rape in classical antiquity is a long one. The rape of Europa by Zeus was experienced as of the essence of religion – not religion as law, with the forms and rituals that support it, but as the central feature of religious life. From that point down to the rape of the Sabine women, where the myth makes room for the externalized image, it is the principal component in the foundation of the city and culture. Of course, when we imagine rape, we cannot omit its primordial and primitive antecedents, with the actual fact of a man sallying forth from his tribe and raping a woman from another tribe. In all its primitiveness, it must be looked upon as the mythical foundation of rape at the origin of culture. Rape lies at the base of the

Greek legacy; because of the profusion of its appearances, we can say it was a source of Greek psychic knowledge; it is fundamental in Homer's *Iliad* and *Odyssey,* whose original inspiration was the rape of Helen, rape with the extremely complicated intervention of the deity resulting in Paris's seduction of Helen, the terrestrial personification of Aphrodite.

Now what we call *psychic rape* is a profoundly important happening that occurs when the myth of rape, in this case the rape of Persephone by Pluto, takes place in the psyche. Because of its archetypal nature, it is impossible to foment or induce, and impossible to mimic. It is a happening in the psychic nature where psychotherapy alone can propitiate the incubation preceding it and reflection on the event itself. This is the only thing that can compensate for hysteria in cases where the personality exhibits what is pathologically considered to be hysteria and in cases of possession. Be this as it may, in the realm of mortals, rape is the psychic impact that deflowers the soul and so opens the doors to mature emotion, the emotion that connects the psyche with the corporeality in which it lives, and with feeling.

But in this approach to hysteria, psychic rape is taken to be that which moves the hysterical state out of a two-dimensional life in which the dominant element is the infernal repetition constantly rebounding from Jung's imaginary platform. The reader should not think that the above has resolved the problem of hysteria once and for all – not by any means. The myth of the suffocation of the daughter by the mother, Demeter suffocating her daughter Persephone, and then Persephone raped by Pluto, are central episodes, to be sure, but episodes in mysterious initiations. So much so that they form part of the Eleusinian mysteries, which is tantamount to saying that hysteria is one of the great mysteries. This leads us to the deeper consideration of a mythologem containing very primitive archaic complexes which are found in clinical pictures dominated by hysteria and the pathologies arising from it. They are complexes which, after the experience of psychic rape, actually transform and produce psychic movements.

We can experience the primitive side of hysteria when suffocation is no longer concealed within the patterns of life and becomes extremely possessive. Anthropology points out that in some primitive societies fathers look on their children as *their* possessions, an attitude that can even lead to them killing their children. This supplies a horrific image of the lengths to which suffocation may go. It may also show us the background to an everyday situation observed as through a magnifying glass in psychotherapy, when suffocation becomes ultra-possessive.

Any experienced psychiatrist or psychotherapist in similar situations has had more than one opportunity to read the genesis of many psychoses and schizophrenias, and a great deal of what is covered by the term psychosomatic disorders. Here I shall quote the case of a female patient who was diagnosed as schizophrenic very early. When I spoke to her mother, she confessed that her attitude to her daughter had always been to protect and guard her "as if she were in a little crystal box." We can cite this verbal image as an example of what I am referring to: suffocation raised to levels of primitive possession. But without going to those extremes, which of us has not known someone in a political, teaching or similar position in whom hysterical suffocation attained possessive, primitive levels and who, in the practice of their profession, exhibited that touch of madness which comes from the most primitive complexes? Thus hysteria, with its multiple and sometimes subtle manifestations, has firm roots in the politician who governs us, the priest who comforts our souls, the doctor who cures our physical ills, the schoolmaster who teaches us, the banker who manages our money and the psychotherapist to whom we relate our psychic conflicts. In all that pertains to the couple as the basic institution of life, we know that hysteria is always present, manifesting itself under some banal pretext in outbursts here and there. Needless to say, many breakups have to do with one member of the couple being no longer able to bear life ruled by hysteria. Observing for many years hysteria which is at the core of the life lived by some couples, a life which the collective consciousness calls 'normal,' demands a certain respect and makes one think again about what could be called the mysteries of a relationship ruled by mutual suffocation. Apart from this, there is no doubt that this possessive trait appears most clearly in medicine and psychotherapy. It shows up when the doctor or psychotherapist talks about the patient as 'his patient' or 'my analysand,' with all the infinite possible variations. This makes it obvious that the practice of medicine or psychotherapy is bogged down in a state of primitive suffocation and that, when suffocation is turned into power, the possibility of therapy being conscious and affecting the occurrence of psychic rape cannot be depended upon.

At the beginning of the century, Jung diagnosed another variety of hysteria that he called *Hebephrenic hysteria.* I think it is relevant to introduce it here in order to enlarge our vision of unusual pathologies and appearances that cloak our access to consciousness of failure. Hebephrenic hysteria is an hysterical state in which infantile traits predominate. Without going too deeply into the complexities of this condition, and using it, as we said before, as a magnifying glass to visualize everyday life, we see that this type of hysteria is more common – we could almost say more 'popular' – than we imagine ... because we sometimes feel that it turns into 'culture.' It could even be said that the culture of the century, in being dominated by naively accepted psychological theories which have focused on childhood for finding the cause of mental illness, has given an unprecedented and exaggerated importance to childhood, resulting in an hysterical exaggeration of the infantile side of the personality. We can now appreciate that the power and guilt released by these theories have created a culture that projects a great deal of hysteria upon the importance of a child's early upbringing: on the importance of a happy childhood as the basis for a healthy life, transformed into a Disneyland to which mental access is easy and constant, nourishing that hebephrenic hysteria. What was said before from the angle of the *puer aeternus* is here being reflected from the angle of hysteria. Whatever picture we can make from Jung's diagnosis of hebephrenic hysteria, either personal or cultural, it is obviously valid.

The cultural aspects introduced here actually come from images in my practice, from a front-row view of Western society and, last but not least, from the obstinacy of the psychological childhood theories dominating the minds of many psychologists. Such psychologists, it seems, retain these theories throughout their life, as if they were in a bunker of power, disregarding the fact that the person they are treating is at an age with a psychic reality very distant from that of childhood. In personalities dominated by hysteria, life is lived according to the hysterical conception, and anything that does not fit in with that illusion lacks all validity. To study and to make the connections between certain types of hysterical personalities and what Jungian psychology calls *fairy-tale psychology* is a task still to be undertaken. We have known personalities in whom the fantasy of the magic castle is carried to extremes, admitting neither discussion nor reflection. The magic castle will always exist in their minds as the only life, and that differentiates them substantially from the cases in which fairy-tale psychology allows reflection and a movement towards more consistent levels of the psyche.

I also want to mention another important conception that might lead us to a more accurate view of the differentiation and relationship between hysteria and *animus*. The *animus* was 'discovered,' so to speak, by Jung and his first generation followers. While aware of its bottomless complexities, for the purposes of my argument here, let us concentrate on the way in which the *animus* is conceived as an instrument of women and its importance in today's world. Many women work in the same conditions and to the same rhythm as men, and the animus is the implement which puts women in our everyday life on a par with men in almost every activity, even those which are historically male preserve. But within the greater complexities it comprises, the *animus* has a particular one that concerns both men and women, appearing in the present-day world in hypertrophied form as a cliché that is nearly always grotesque. It is the 'opinion-expressing' aspect of the *animus*.

We live in a world of opinions that influence and cover every aspect of our daily life. Present-day man attaches great importance to them, for they affect not only his eating habits and his sex life, but also his relation to the society in which he lives. They even influence his customs and habits to the point of altering or destroying his most personal family and religious traditions. Though we may be striving for consciousness, it is superficial notions conceived from the pseudo-logos of the *animus* that we swallow and transmit to our way of life. The fact is that this 'opinion-expressing' aspect of the *animus* often appears as a possessive element. We see personalities who are possessed, not by unconscious or irrational forces of archetypal provenance, but by opinions which they are prepared to defend to the last. I think it is easy to see how these opinions combine perfectly with hysterical suffocation, and that suffocation is not wholly confined within the archetypal limits we mentioned, but works also in an alarming way through the medium of opinions.

We feel that we are living in times of tremendous hysteria and at the same time of tremendous exaggeration, that our human life has, in a very few years, become more exaggerated than at any time in humanity's past history. Man's recent history has increased hysteria to what are sometimes frightening proportions, especially when we know that hysteria covers a spectrum of human nature ranging from what every mother does archetypally; i.e., suffocate her daughter, to a figure who easily accommodates all the evil the human race attributes to him – Adolf Hitler.

It was not without reason that the word 'hysteria' was eliminated from the medical terminology of the American Psychiatric Association and replaced by 'conversion.' This is tantamount to saying that the hysterical phenomenon is only taken into account and treated medically when it appears as a phenomenon of conversion. At the same time, however, it is saying that the majority of the infinite hysterical manifestations with which everyday life teems pass beyond the bounds of the screen of psychiatric conception, which usually undervalues and despises them. Thus they are submerged in the collective unconsciousness, and from there, they impregnate our life at the most everyday banal levels to such a degree that the fate of humanity depends on them, so to speak, even if that sounds a bit hysterical. For there can be no doubt that our life is growing more and more hysterical every day; we have only to study any of the so-called media, now hypertrophied by TV, to sense how the elements of hysterical complexes are force-fed pablum ranging from a naive soap ad to superpowers confronting each other with nuclear weapons.

The connection we made earlier between hysteria and fairy tale shows up the superficiality of hysteria very clearly, but we feel the same superficiality when we read the most horrifying news about the superpowers, their armaments and their potential for destruction. It is not surprising that the apathy about such important matters found by some writers in modern man is accompanied by a powerful dose of hysteria, and that when they actually reach us, they are caught on Jung's imaginary platform, which blocks their passage to the hysterical complexes and archetypes, and of course to our instincts, which are what should really react. We pick up a newspaper and read stories about a celebrity, a sports event, a national disaster or the number of missiles some power or other possesses, all on the same superficial hysterical level. There is hardly any difference in the values attached to each item; it seems as if everything is reduced to hysterical information intended to feed our hysteria.

This magical, fairy-tale superficiality of hysteria is an everyday occurrence in psychotherapy and can be used by us as a magnifying glass. Through it we see how impossible it is for situations, problems and obvious psychic contents to be accepted with the required reality and to touch the psyche emotionally, or for the psyche to feel moved by them. We see (and it shocks our sensibility) that pains, grief and tragedy are swept away in an instant by hysteria. Eliot's line, "Humankind cannot bear very much reality ...," is apposite here. For the purposes of this discussion, however, it is also pertinent to say that the hysterical personality, the hysterical component of each individual and the collective hysterias contrive, with staggering superficiality, to evade the basic reality we have mentioned, which would make possible acceptance of the consciousness of failure and the psychic lesson that goes with it.

I hope the reader is bearing in mind the limitations of this brief disquisition on hysteria, although it does embody an archetypal view of the subject, and that alone is something new. The archetypal view affords us a better appreciation of the metaphor applied to it: "It has more shapes than Proteus and more colors than the chameleon." A description that sums up the inaccessibility, the intangibility, of hysteria, as well as the mysterious spectrum already mentioned. Within the mystery, we have to admit that hardly anything is known of the function – the why and wherefore – of hysteria in our nature (provided that we do not cling hysterically to superficial reductions). I think that establishing it as a constituent part of our nature is a perfectly valid step, but when all is said and done, the mystery remains: the archetypal mystery of the Eleusinian mysteries.

But another important feature of hysteria is that it is able to adopt any instrument and use it as a vehicle for manifesting itself. Apparently one of the most readily available instruments, which fits hysteria like a glove, is guilt-making. Consequently, we sometimes have the spectacle of hysteria using guilt-making, with subtlety and insinuation, and sometimes we are embarrassed by its barefaced effrontery. This brings us closer to knowing by experience why hysteria is so important to my theme, because, if hysteria manipulates guilt with its characteristic skill, I assert that it has at its disposal an infinite spectrum of possibilities for blaming anyone about anything and consequently does not accept consciousness of failure. By imputing guilt, hysteria destroys the image of the psychic happening.

The third element that does not recognize failure is the one comprised in the concept of 'personality disorders,' which in this study, to give them a rather broader meaning, we regard as psychopathic components of the personality. They are components of every human being, though they are not archetypal, a fact that already characterizes them more specifically and indicates their dangerous nature. Not being archetypal, they naturally lack image and form; they burst into the personality without rhyme or reason as manifestations of excess and immoderation. They are in radical opposition to the archetypal forms of living because, as I have said, they are elements without form. But allow me to elaborate a little: If we conceive of something with forms, those forms impose from the outset a limit. Now, if we make the effort to conceive of a component that we all possess without forms (for we really have to make an effort to arrive at such a concept), what emerges instead of form with limits is excess. And it is in the study of personalities whose dominant component is excess that we acquire some degree of experience of that part of ourselves. It is extremely difficult to admit that the excessive psychopath who figures in history and confronts us every day in newspapers and periodicals, and as a cinema hero, etc., is in all of us. It is tantamount to saying – and not only saying, but also to conceiving experientially – that this evil takes up its abode or is already present in each one of us. I accept the foregoing as extreme, following the definition of the word 'psychopath' in textbooks on psychopathology, but I also see it as being part of human nature, a point emphasized throughout this study. Here, however, I want to look on it in a rather more mundane way, if such a thing is possible. I want to bring it up as an important element which forms the worst barrier to consciousness of failure. For if the psychopath himself has no form, he cannot recognize form of any kind and naturally cannot conceive of failure, still less be conscious of it.

I should like to give the reader a portrait of the psychopath (or the psychopathic component existing in all of us). To this end, allow me to borrow from the same material in modern literature that I took in the first essay of the book in my discussion on Titanism: *The Clockwork Orange* and *The Outsider*. *The Clockwork Orange,* that masterly book by Anthony Burgess, shows a world in which the psychopath rules unchecked. Life is lived in total excess; there are neither limits nor forms. The established entities that might provide forms and limits, such as religion, the state, etc., are also possessed by the same excess, as if excess had wiped out all the accepted forms on which life is based. In the book, psychiatry also turns out to be an expression of excess by trying to cure technologically something that, if described in terms of clinical diagnosis, would be lack of soul – and that is the psychopathic personality in essence. Where there should be soul, psyche, experience of life, intuition and a sense of personal values, there is only a *lacuna,* nothing; someone without heart or soul.

Burgess's book confronts us with the horror and danger of the psychopathic, of the excess which is expressed not only in the extreme forms described in *The Clockwork Orange,* but is also, to a lesser degree, at large in all of us, though better hidden, and at times disguised, as good intentions. The study of a psychopathic personality or a psychopathic component is perhaps the greatest challenge to current psychological and psychiatric studies – studies made extremely difficult by the very lack of form of the subject being studied and which become more and more laborious if we tackle them from the traditional viewpoint. But nowadays any self-respecting psychotherapist knows that he must have some idea of what I am talking about and must also be aware that it is necessary to fight as fiercely and as radically as possible with the psychopathic component. If he fails to do so, if he fails in reflecting it, then that psychopathic component itself will waylay, attack and denature his psychotherapeutic standpoint; it will discredit or sweep aside his therapeutical work. In this business of psychotherapy, the age has stuffed us with theories, which at best serve as points of reference. Many of them are mere schemas and naturally contain a good dose of myopia or even blindness, of which the psychopathic titan can take advantage to make his appearance: psychological theories which the titan has made use of and are mimetic instruments in his hands. The fact is that the titan claims to practise psychotherapy based on theories he is dying to apply, but without the remotest conception that the happening of psychotherapy is a product of the psyche itself, of the psychic interrelation between therapist and patient, and that theories (any kind of theory) are irrelevant and in most cases obstruct the natural occurrence of the psyche.

That is why I prefer to seek support in literature and the reflection supplied by mythology and use their contributions as more pliable and imaginative instruments. Thus we turn again to another modern masterpiece, *The Outsider,* by Albert Camus, which tells us about the outsider we all have within us. The title of the book alone indicates its subject: someone alien to ourselves. Camus's book also offers us the direct, vivid and deeply experienced dramatization of the psychopath's internal void, the lack of inner forms in Mersault, the personification of the outsider. The first page never fails to surprise us when we read about Mersault receiving a telegram announcing his mother's death, without showing any kind of response that such news would normally elicit.

The reader must forgive me for repeating these two examples from modern literature, previously referred to in my essay on "Moon Madness – Titanic Love." I prefer to consider them as variations on the same theme rather than repetitions, my reason being that, although I could easily cite other examples, none of them would have been as convincing as either of these two novels. My aim is to emphasize what I feel to be of essential interest, because the subject is so foreign to current values that our best hope is to make use of the characters who can help us to grasp it, what we want to apprehend being highly inaccessible, because it has no forms. Bearing this in mind, I refer the reader to Luchino Visconti, who makes this a basic theme, with very rich variations, throughout his cinematographic *œuvre.*

I trust that this brief sketch will help the reader to understand that, when it functions in excess and does not adapt itself to limits or forms, the psychopathic component proves beyond doubt that there are inner flaws in human nature. The excess of the psychopath does not belong to any archetype, nor is it subject to any form. As we see in *The Outsider,* the flaw that appears on the first page shows that the archetype of the mother, here to be seen as a two-headed (mother-son, son-mother) archetype, seems not to exist. By referring to the works quoted, I want to give the reader a vivid practical vision of the psychopathic personality from both the inside and the outside, a vision giving easier access to the infinitely cruel realities of the human being. Having done so, I can leave these enormously complex subjects and confine myself to what I have to say about mimetism which, in my view, is essential to the study of psychopathy, both when it dominates the personality and when it is regarded as a component.

The psychopath is the living expression of the phrase – "there's nothing inside them" – that we sometimes apply to people. Everything is external, borrowed and captured by facile processes. In this mimetism of the outside world, the psychopathic personality or the psychopathic component adapts itself to the event with which it is faced. We all need a certain degree of mimetism, and that is apparently why nature endows us with it. We need mimetism to adapt ourselves to extreme situations that are alien to us. But in present-day societies (the history of our time) there is undoubtedly a notable increase of the pressing need for adaptation to the external world. That may be why such components have become so hypertrophied. We are constantly meeting with things we cannot understand because, although they excite us and, in being everyday occurrences we have to learn to adapt to them, they are still too alien to our learning process. This results in the more immediate histrionics of hysteria and facile psychopathic mimicry, two instruments that history has developed for us, out of necessity. From this aspect, it seems that Western man has acquired a degree of consciousness stemming from his classical heritage (Plato discussed our subject in his *Timaeus*). Given a soul with its archetypes, images, forms and intelligence, there is also Necessity (*ananke*), which we need in order to respond to something that has no form known to us. The responses are infinite and can range from mimetism (in order to come to terms with an unfamiliar situation) to extremes of evil. The old saying, "When in Rome, do as the Romans do," is relevant here – or as a friend of mine said, "If I were parachuted into China, I would have to do something to survive, and the first idea to come into my head would be to smile like the Chinese." This is a humorous and self-evident example of what Timaeus called Necessity in this 5th-century Athenian discourse, but it also clearly shows the superficial absurdity of this necessity. To the Chinese, the smile comes from within; a smile, so the experts say, which is a language in itself, with an age-old tradition that can express even wisdom. This is tantamount to saying that no matter how hard my friend tried to smile like a Chinaman, his smile would be a pale echo that at best might just ensure his survival among the Chinese.

Forgive me for using a Chinese anecdote as a somewhat colloquial image to give access to the profound thinking in the *Timaeus,* but I feel very deeply that what I am talking about here are urgent necessities of our times. Woody Allen, the American film actor and director, conveys this in his film *Zelig* which, using imagery full of historicity, portrays the reflection of mimicry carried to the extremes of total autonomy. Zelig mimics everything he sees, but within the resultant comedy our attention is aroused when we see that Zelig even goes so far as to mimic Adolf Hitler. And there we see the actor's audacious intentions achieving what we are concerned with here: two extremes of the personality which is known as psychopathic in modern psychiatric terminology, ranging from adaptive mimetism for survival to evil.

History has developed these elements for us out of necessity, but at the expense of our archetypal world of forms and, why not say it, of the loss of soul. By soul I mean here the registering of the event of living internally and emotionally. We live in a world where Necessity reaches man through communication media, but as the name implies, these media make him mediocre, transmitting only the demands of what Timaeus called Necessity, a necessity that is growing and systematically destroying the remains of Western man's personal values, and, in the process his feeling, his emotions and his privacy.

As a result, the dominant countries on the world stage today are the most mimetic. We have only to think of a country with incredible mimetic ability, such as Japan, and how overnight it dominated technology, that daughter of Necessity, of which Aeschylus was already aware. This means that today technology, something native to the West, presents us with the absurd picture of a nation completely alien to Western culture mimicking and dominating that field. What can also be seen, which is even more absurd, is the excessive greed of the West, which in turn tries to mimic Japanese technology – to mimic what has already been mimicked – to play technological mimicry as a trump card.

Hence we can understand that both hysterical histrionics and psychopathic mimetism are legal and immediately effective currency in the attempt to 'succeed' in whatever we may like to call modern society. And we begin to feel how, of these components, one of which is characterized by its superficiality, the other by its excess, the latter, emerging from a void, a nothingness, turns out to be the more significant. These components also tell us that their only goal is success, that the values of that success are not even remotely relevant, and that whatever we may think of them, we instantly realize that they are bound to block any access to consciousness of failure.

This feeling stems from the knowledge that consciousness of failure is internal and obscure. When using the term, we are not referring to something we can read through easily accessible schemas. Consciousness of failure belongs (and I think we are beginning to understand this) to obscure areas in which our inwardness moves. When we speak of consciousness of failure we are speaking of those slow median states of the soul, *Anima media natura,* because in this state of soul there is no mad craving for success, simply because there is a psyche that is conscious, that does not conceive of the accelerations necessary for the conceptions of the *puer,* nor the hysterical histrionics, nor the psychopathic mimetism. This is a soul that does not suffer the torments of being success-oriented, but also a soul that is unshaken by the opposite pole, failure turned into reality; the failure that sometimes appears and stubbornly repeats the boring refrain: "I feel that I am a failure – I've failed" – with that note of hysterical and depressive psychopathic repetition, in addition to being a failure projected outwards – an "I feel I'm a failure" which really says: "I feel I'm a failure because I haven't been able to achieve the goals of modern, success-oriented slogans." Consciousness of failure is something else; it is something more precious and highly psychic; it is evasive – it comes and goes – and in addition, it asserts its mercurial characteristics. It is a median obscure consciousness, as I have already said; its rightful place is on the threshold and its light is crepuscular. But this is the position from which we reconcile ourselves to our mortal limitations, and in so doing, we fit into the best defined limits of our being and into what we are in reality, into what facilitates the image with its potential for a cultured life.

Coming to terms with the consciousness of failure, we inadvertently enter the field of the image, and the image, in a poet's words, is possibility. To quote a splendid line of Lezama Lima's: "The hypothesis of the image is possibility." And the possibilities are those of imagery, that which makes the office of the image-maker possible, though this ability to form images is a limited earthly activity by virtue of its own consistent archetypal limits. But like Lezama, what I mean by limitation is *superabundance.* It is paradoxical. As soon as we speak of images, we begin to speak of superabundance, all the more so if we admit that a single image is more than enough to fill our whole existence. From the moment the image to which we belong begins to emerge, there is an enriched but very remote psychic movement, since it has absolutely no connection with psychopathic-cum-titanic repetitiveness. It is worthy of repetition that "The hypothesis of the image is possibility"; the image that makes us possible, and within the possibility of the image we are a little distant, though never immune, from the unbearable horror of those two opposites – success and failure. It is in and from the image that we find the repose of the opposites, success and failure.

In the Jungian psychology of opposites, art is understood as an attempt to compensate for collective consciousness, because an art concerned with reconciling itself to the collective consciousness displays its own superficiality, and if we accept it, we do so knowing its limits. We should also realize that this is how psychotherapy should be experienced, and there is, therefore, an affinity between the poet and the psychotherapist: psychotherapy understood as craftsmanship and art. This also serves as a means of contrast so that we can assess our feelings when some artistic happening or artifact stirs us to our depths and compensates for the tedium, boredom and horror of the collective consciousness.

But art needs independence and privacy, as well as a certain consciousness which encourages that contact bordering on the poetic. The act of creating a work of art moves us by its economy. All that a poet needs is a pencil and paper. A painter needs a little more; paints, brushes, a canvas. Both poet and painter can be left alone with the tools of their trade, and hear and feel what they want to express through them. I draw attention to this economy because I feel that the psychic world, the experience of soul, reveals itself to us with similar economy. The moment we are capable of psychically evaluating the experience of soul, we are getting a little closer to what is called a crisis of the soul. We approach, and try to adapt ourselves a little better to the wide range of depressions, and it is then that we start to live, feel and value the depths. The slow movements of depression are the only way (today we can say with absolute certainty that they are the *via regia*) to what we call psychic creativity.

At this point, I must introduce a poem by Rafael Cadenas, entitled *Failure [Fracaso]*. It came into my life giving form, beautiful poetic form, to thoughts and ideas which have been with me for many years and which I experienced as a consciousness of failure. Now, thanks to what we call art, I have found an appropriate form to express the deepest inner experience. It is offered to us with exemplary generosity:

Everything I've taken for victory is only smoke.

Failure, background language, track from a more demanding
    space, it's difficult to read between your lines.

When you branded my forehead, I never thought about the
    message you delivered, more precious than any triumph.

Your flaming face has pursued me and I did not know it was to
    save me.

You have kept me on the sidelines for my own good, you denied
    me easy accomplishments, you've closed doors to me.

It was I you wanted to defend by not letting me shine.

Out of sheer love for me you've dealt with the emptiness that so many nights has made me speak feverishly to a woman who was never there.

To protect me you've let others pass me by, you've made women choose someone more determined, you kept me away from suicidal tasks.

You have always come to the rescue.

Yes, your ulcerated body, spat on, hated, has received me in my purest form to deliver me to the clarity of the desert.

Out of madness I've cursed you, abused you, and said blasphemous things about you.

You don't exist.

You've been invented out of delirious pride.

How much I owe you!

You promoted me to a higher rank wiping me clean with a rough sponge, hurling me onto my true battlefield, giving me the weapons that triumph leaves behind.

You've led me by the hand to the only water that reflects me.

Because of you I do not know the anxiety of acting out a role, of maintaining a position by force, of climbing up by my own effort, of fighting for a higher rank, of expanding myself to the point of exploding.

You've made me humble, quiet, rebellious.

I don't praise you for what you are, but for what you've kept me from becoming. For not giving me another life. For having limited me.

You've given only nakedness.

It's true you've taught harshly, and you yourself cauterized me. But you also gave me the joy of not fearing you.

Thank you for trading my density in exchange for my thick handwriting.

Thank you for keeping me from getting a swelled head.

Thank you for the riches you have forced on me.

Thank you for building my house with clay.

Thank you for setting me apart.

Thank you.

Rafael Cadenas' poem is the only written work I know that really tallies with the insights that have been gestating inside me for years (what I have called 'consciousness of failure' in this paper). The poem shows us how just one man, with just one poem, can compensate for all the success-oriented excess which surrounds us. From the outset, it demonstrates that failure is a 'language of the depths'; it states clearly that consciousness of it comes from below, from realms of depression to which historical repression condemned it. It exists in these depths, in these realms of our own being, in these different regions and illuminations which are harder to interpret and experience. We may call it depression, but let us note that the consciousness which emerges from this depression appears like a precious jewel. Moreover, it is not something we can look on as a bauble sold on the open market, but rather a jewel beautifully crafted in the soul and worth so many carats, that, put in the scales, it might be equated with salvation. Cadenas appeals for salvation through consciousness of failure, and in the process, he is undoubtedly remitting us to our own depths. He makes this very clear when he is pursued by the god who burns and saves. We are pursued by something that is so foreign to our conscious nature that it is difficult to accept or tolerate it. Consciousness is unknowing and fearful, and a flaming face can only cause fear. Nevertheless, that is how the gods disguise themselves, and here the image is unequivocal: with horror comes salvation. "Your flaming face has pursued me, and I did not know it was to save me." Salvation comes from accepting horror, and failure begins to impose the very precise limits which are adjusted to the configuration of a personality in a state of consciousness of failure: "You have kept me on the sidelines for my own good, you denied me easy accomplishments, you've closed doors to me."

There is another line which fits in perfectly with the foregoing, when the poet says: "You've made women choose someone more determined ..." Here the poet offers the basis for an essential differentiation between the man who is related to women who are attracted to success and the *Anima Media*

Natura referred to above, the woman we all carry within us, who is simultaneously our soul companion. She is a woman who does not hurl herself at someone more determined, who does not yield herself to victory or success, but continues to enjoy her median nature; an anima who does not push us towards success, but who keeps us from "suicidal tasks," from suicidal depressions. When Cadenas says of consciousness of failure – "You have always come to the rescue ..." – he is transmitting a feeling of trust, as if that consciousness were the only thing to trust in. In Spanish this is a very taurine line – *"tu siempre has venido al quite"* – full of the coloring that comes from the fiesta. A *quite* is made when there are moments of danger during a bullfight. When we are in highly dangerous situations, it is consciousness of failure which performs the *quite* for us. In bullfighting, the *quite* is traditionally looked on as the intervention of Divine Providence. For there are *quites* when the cape seems to be wielded by the hand of Providence and saves the bullfighter from imminent danger. That is how the poet sees failure, as saving him from danger. Even at this point we feel as if consciousness of failure were an inner movement completed in profound realities, in naked truths and the apotheosis of joy.

The reader must forgive my temerity in expressing the profound effect that some lines from Rafael Cadenas' poem have had on me, but in so doing, I believe I am communicating the great joy I felt when I came across *Fracaso*: joy that is affirmed and lived in a state of higher consciousness, which comes to us from the profound consciousness of failure. It is difficult to find another line that expresses our reality so accurately as Cadenas': "I don't praise you for what you are, but for what you've kept me from becoming. For not giving me another life. For having limited me."

This is the reality of individuation, the adaptation of oneself, confined within one's own proper boundaries. Here, as Cadenas says, "You've given only nakedness ..." – reality confined and naked truth. The reality and truth indispensable for feeling joy. Joy that is inner apotheosis in Cadenas, brightening up the inner world that makes consciousness of failure possible. Joy that can be felt as a higher consciousness holding joy and failure in a paradoxical embrace.

BIBLIOGRAPHY

Burkert, Walter, "The Great Gods, Adonis and Hippolytus." In *History in Greek Mythology and Ritual.* University of California Press, Berkeley, California, 1982.

Cadenas, Rafael, *Los Cuadernos del Destierro. Falsas Maniobras. Derrota.* Editorial Fundarte, Caracas, 1979.

Guggenbuhl-Craig, Adolf, *Eros on Crutches.* Spring Publications, University of Dallas, Texas, 1980.

Jung, C.G., *Psychiatric Studies.* In The Collected Works, Vol. I, Routledge & Kegan Paul Ltd., London, 1957.

Kerényi, Karl, *Eleusis – Archetypal Image of Mother and Daughter.* Bollingen Series LXV 4, Bollingen Foundation, New York, 1967.

Lezama Lima, José, *Las Eras Imaginarias.* Edit. Fudamentos, Madrid, 1971.

Micklem, Neil, *On Hysteria: The Mythical Syndrome.* In Spring, 1974. Spring Publications, Zurich 1974.

Sheldon, William, *Prometheus Revisited.* Schenkman Publishing Company, Cambridge, Massachusetts, 1975.

von Franz, Marie-Louise, *Puer Aeternus.* Spring Publications Inc., Dallas, Texas, 1976.

Ziegler, Alfred J., *Archetypal Medicine.* Spring Publications Inc., Dallas, Texas, 1983.

OTHER RECENT TITLES FROM DAIMON:

C.A. Meier
HEALING DREAM AND RITUAL
Ancient Incubation and modern Psychotherapy

ca. 170 pages; paper; 10 illustrations, indexes
ISBN 3-85630-510-6

C.A. Meier calls for modern psychotherapy to honor the role that the dream has played in the healing process, from ancient times to the present.

Healing Dream and Ritual is one of the most significant and lasting witnesses of how far beyond immediate psychology the implications of Jung's work stretches. This book is, in my feeling, as important for today's healers as was the early work of Paracelsus to the redirection of medicine in the Renaissance.

Sir Laurens van der Post

Rafael López-Pedraza
HERMES AND HIS CHILDREN
illustrations; 220 pages; paper
ISBN 3-85630-518-1

Hermes and his Children was originally published in 1977 and quickly became something of a classic among therapists, poets, artists and readers of every ilk around the world.

Rafael López-Pedraza approaches the soul through myth, pathology, image and the very living of them all.

The love and passion of a man fully in his element radiates throughout this unique work, now updated and expanded for this edition.

Rafael López-Pedraza was born in Cuba in 1920 of Spanish heritage. He lived in Zurich from 1963 until 1974 and attended the C.G. Jung Institute. Today he lives in Caracas, Venezuela, where he divides his time between professorial duties, a psychotherapeutic practice and writing.

ENGLISH PUBLICATIONS BY **DAIMON**

The Savage and Beautiful Country, Alan McGlashan
A Testament to the Wilderness, Ed. by R. Hinshaw
Talking with Angels, (transcribed by Gitta Mallasz)
A Time to Mourn, Verena Kast
Imprints of the Future, George Czuczka
Healing Dream and Ritual, C.A. Meier
Meetings with Jung, E.A. Bennet
Life Paints its own Span, Susan Bach
The Myth of Meaning, Aniela Jaffé
Was C.G. Jung a Mystic? Aniela Jaffé
From the Life and Work of C.G. Jung, Aniela Jaffé
Friedrich Nietzsche, Liliane Frey-Rohn

Jungian Congress Papers:

Jerusalem 1983: *Symbolic and Clinical Approaches*
Ed. by Luigi Zoja, R. Hinshaw

Berlin 1986: *The Archetype of Shadow in a Split World*
Ed. by M.-A. Mattoon

Available from your bookstore or from our distributors:

All territories
Daimon Verlag
Am Klosterplatz
CH-8840 Einsiedeln
Switzerland
Tel. (55) 53 22 66

Great Britain
Element Books Ltd.
Longmead Shaftesbury
Dorset SP7 8PL
England
Tel. (0747) 51 339

U.S.A.
Inland Book Company
P.O. Box 261
East Haven, Conn. 06512
(800) 243 01 38

U.S.A. West
The Great Tradition
750 Adrian Way,
Suite 111
San Rafael, CA 94903
Tel. (415) 492 93 82